Problem Regions of Europe
General Editor **D. I. Scargill**

The Massif Central
Hugh Clout

OXFORD UNIVERSITY PRESS

Oxford University Press, Walton Street, Oxford OX2 6DP

Oxford   London   Glasgow
New York   Toronto   Melbourne   Wellington
Kuala Lumpur   Singapore   Jakarta   Hong Kong   Tokyo
Delhi   Bombay   Calcutta   Madras   Karachi
Ibadan   Nairobi   Dar es Salaam   Cape Town

© Oxford University Press 1973

First published 1973
Reprinted 1974 and 1978 (with revision)

Filmset by BAS Printers Limited, Over Wallop, Hampshire
and printed in Great Britain
at the University Press, Oxford
by Vivian Ridler, Printer to the University

Editor's Preface

Great economic and social changes have taken place in Europe in recent years. The agricultural labour force has almost everywhere contracted, in some places very rapidly, and the lack of alternative forms of employment in rural areas has resulted in large-scale movements of farmers and farm labourers in search of work in the cities. The scale of this drift from the land can be gauged from the fact that in the six (original) Common Market countries the agricultural work force was halved between 1950 and 1970: from approximately 20 millions to 10 millions. In many areas this rural exodus has made it possible to carry out much needed reorganization of farm holdings, but it has also brought with it problems concerning, for example, the provision of services to a contracting population and the need to establish new forms of land use where farming is no longer profitable.

Contraction of the labour force has also taken place in several old-established industries. These include coal-mining, shipbuilding, and the more traditional textile industries, where the effects of a shrinking market have been made more severe by automation, which has substituted machines for men. The coal-mining industry of Western Europe shed something like two-thirds of its labour force during the 1950s and 1960s. Wherever a large proportion of the working population was dependent upon a declining industry of this kind, the problems of adjustment have been severe. Many schemes have been devised to attract alternative forms of employment but, despite incentives, it has often proved difficult to attract new firms because of the old industrial areas' legacy of dirt, derelict landscape, poor housing, and, in some places, bad labour relations.

Problems of a different kind have arisen as a result of the continued growth of large cities such as London and Paris, or of groups of closely related cities as in the case of Randstad Holland. The reasons for such growth are several. To the manufacturer the big city offers the advantage of a local market, a varied labour force, and easy access to suppliers and other manufacturers with whom he needs to maintain close links. To them and even more to the service industries a city location offers a prestige location, and the enormous expansion of service activity, especially office-work, has contributed greatly to postwar urban growth. Attempts to control the increase of employment within cities have had some success as far as manufacturing industry is concerned but very little with regard to office work.

Problems resulting from city growth include traffic congestion, high land prices, pollution, and social stress brought about by factors such as housing shortages and travelling long distances to work. Yet the city continues to attract migrants for whom the image is still one of streets paved with gold, whilst the established resident is loath to leave the 'bright lights', the football club, or the familiar shops.

Geographers, in the past, have been reluctant to focus their attention on regional problems. The problem was thought to be a temporary phenomenon and therefore less worthy of consideration than regional characteristics of a more enduring nature—the landscape or the chimerical *personality* of the region. Yet such is the magnitude, persistence, and areal extent of problems of the kind referred to above that the geographer would seem to be well justified in approaching his regional study by seeking to identify, measure, and even seek solutions to problems.

'Devenant alors un cadre de recherche, la région sera choisie en fonction de certains problèmes et des moyens qui permettent de les aborder avec profit' (H. Baulig). Indeed it has been suggested that regions can be defined in terms of the problems with which they are confronted.

Additional stimulus for studying regional problems arises from the interest which politicians and planners have recently shown in the region as a framework for tackling such issues as the relief of unemployment, the siting of new investment, and the reorganization of administrative boundaries. Governments have long been aware of the problems resulting from economic and social changes and various attempts have been made to solve them. Development Areas and New Towns in Great Britain, for example, represent an attempt to deal with the problems, on the one hand, of the declining industrial areas and, on the other, of the overgrown cities. Such solutions can hardly be described as regional, however. Other countries have recognized the problems of their over-populated rural areas and the Cassa per il

Mezzogiorno, the Fund for the South, was set up by the Italian government in 1950 in order to encourage investment in the South. The E.E.C. has also channelled funds via its Investment Bank, both to southern Italy and to other parts of the Common Market distant from the main centres of economic activity. Planning of this kind shows an awareness of the regional extent of economic and social problems, though in practice much of the actual work of planning was undertaken on a piecemeal, local, and short-term basis.

Since about 1960, however, the continuing nature of the problems has persuaded most European governments to adopt longer-term and more comprehensive planning measures, and the importance of seeking regional solutions has been increasingly stressed. The last ten years have, in fact, witnessed the setting up of regional planning authorities in many European countries and to them has been given the task of identifying regional problems and of finding solutions to them. A large number of reports have been published following research carried out by these authorities, and individual governments have introduced regional considerations to national planning. The French *métropoles d'équilibre,* for example, were devised in order to introduce new vigour to the regions via the largest provincial towns.

One of the drawbacks to regional planning of this kind is the outdated nature of local government boundaries, most planning decisions having to be implemented through a system of local government more suited to nineteenth than to late twentieth century conditions. Some experts have thus advocated a regional alternative to existing local government areas, and it is interesting to note that the Royal Commission on Local Government in England (the Maud Report), whilst not supporting so radical a change, nevertheless introduced the idea of *provinces* within which broad planning policies could be carried out. Supporters of the regional idea argue that a growing trend toward State centralization is bringing about a reaction in the form of renewed popular interest in regions, their history, industrial archaeology, customs, dialect, and so on.

The revival of interest in regions, both for their own sake and as a practical aid to planning or administration, makes particularly timely the appearance of a series of geographical studies concerned with *Problem Regions of Europe.* The present volume is one of 12 studies comprising such a series.

The twelve regions have been selected in order to illustrate, between them, a variety of problems. The most obvious of these are: problems of a harsh environment, of isolation, of industrial decay, of urban congestion, and of proximity to a sensitive political frontier. One or other of these major problems forms the dominant theme in each of the volumes of the series, but they have not been studied in isolation. Where it has been thought relevant to do so, authors have drawn attention to similar problems encountered in other parts of the continent so that readers may compare both the causes of problems and the methods employed to solve them. At the same time it is recognized that every region has a number of problems that are unique to itself and these peculiarly local problems have been distinguished from those of a more general kind.

Although the precise treatment of each subject will vary according to the nature of the region concerned and, to some extent, the outlook of a particular author, readers will find much in common in the arrangement of contents in each volume. In each of them the nature of the problem or problems which characterize the region is first stated by the author; next the circumstances that have given rise to the problems are explained; after this the methods that have been employed to overcome the problems are subjected to critical examination and evaluation. Each study includes indications of likely future developments.

All the authors of the series have considerable first-hand knowledge of the regions about which they have written. Yet none of them would claim to have a complete set of answers to any particular regional problem. For this reason, as well as from a desire to make the series challenging, each volume contains suggestions for further lines of inquiry that the reader may pursue. The series was conceived initially as one that would be helpful to sixth-form geographers but it is believed that individual volumes will also provide a useful introduction to the detailed work undertaken by more advanced students both of geography and of European studies in general.

D.I.S.

St. Edmund Hall,
August 1972

4

Contents

Acknowledgements

The author wishes to record his thanks to Professor André Fel and his colleagues at the University of Clermont-Ferrand, to Mademoiselle Arveuf and her staff at the Mission Régionale de l'Auvergne, and to rural planners of the Société pour la Mise en Valeur de l'Auvergne-Limousin for providing valuable documentary material and introducing him to many of the social and economic problems of the Massif Central.

The maps in this book have been simplified from other sources as follows:

Fig. 1, Fig. 2, Fig. 3, and Fig. 8 from ESTIENNE, P. & JOLY, R., *La Région du Centre* (Presses Universitaires de France, Paris 1961).

Fig. 5, Fig. 12 from a school textbook entitled *France et Mondes d'Outre-Mer* by BARON, E. & MADRE, J. (Editions de l'Ecole, Paris 1963).

Fig. 6 from an article by ESTIENNE, P 'Etat de nos connaissances géographiques sur le Massif Central français', in *Revue d'Auvergne*, 1958, 72, p. 21.

Fig. 7 from DERRUAU-BONNIOL, S. & FEL, A., *Le Massif Central* (Presses Universitaires de France, 1963).

Fig. 10 from an article by ESTIENNE, P. 'Un demi-siècle de dépeuplement rural dans le Massif Central' in *Revue de Géographie Alpine*, 1958, 46, pp. 463–72.

Fig. 11 from Michelin publicity.

Fig. 13 from the *Agro-Ecological Atlas of Cereal Growing in Europe*, vol. 1, Elsevier, Brockhuizen.

Fig. 15 from the article by SCHNETZLER, J. (1966) quoted in the Further Work, with some additions.

Fig. 16 from ESTIENNE, P. & DERRUAU, S. *Clermont-Ferrand, Notes et Etudes Documentaires*, no. 3221, Paris 1965.

1 The Massif Central in a European Context

Types of 'problem region' in Europe today

By far the greater part of Europe's population lived in the countryside and worked on the land before the industrial revolution. Most towns were very small and movement over long distances was difficult. The majority of people spent the whole of their lives where they had been born. Their world was made up of their home village, the nearest market town, and a few other surrounding settlements. Since 1800 industrialization and urban growth have taken place at different rates in the various parts of the Continent and have now reached differing stages of development. North-west Europe is highly urbanized and industrialized. Only 4 per cent of the British labour force is employed in farming and forestry. In West Germany the figure is 10 per cent and in France 16 per cent. By contrast, the countries of south-east Europe are still far more rural in character, with over 40 per cent of their labour forces working on the land.

There are of course very important regional contrasts in urbanization and industrial development in individual countries and as a result four main types of economic region are found in modern Europe.

At one extreme there are *dynamic* regions which have experienced continuous population growth, urbanization and industrial development since the mid-nineteenth century. South-east England, Randstad Holland, and Paris are perhaps the best examples. In a now famous book, entitled *Paris et le désert français* (1947), J. F. Gravier drew the attention of the French people to the massive growth of their capital city and the relative poverty of the rest of France. Economic and social 'deserts' exist in provincial parts of other European countries as well. Metropolitan regions have become almost completely urbanized and contain few agricultural workers. But in spite of their continuing economic dynamism they must be recognized as 'problem regions' since large numbers of people are crowded into tightly-packed city-regions. Planners have devised management schemes to modernize and enlarge these cities to provide decent conditions for people who already live and work there; and also to accommodate inevitable increases in population and jobs in the future. A third objective involves attempts to decentralize factories and offices to the provinces so that new forms of employment may be provided in the economic 'deserts'.

At the other extreme there are *backward* regions which are still predominantly agricultural and rural in character. Average incomes are low. Southern Italy forms the most extensive backward region in Western Europe but upland areas from the Scottish Highlands to the Pyrenees also come in this category of problem region. Agricultural modernization is hampered by poor soils, harsh climatic conditions, and the old-fashioned attitudes held by many of the inhabitants. Backward regions have been unable to industrialize and develop urban centres sufficiently rapidly over the last hundred years to retain their population. Large numbers of people have migrated to more favourable regions offering better job prospects and higher incomes. The main planning objectives in backward areas involve modernizing agriculture and diversifying economic activities by the introduction of jobs in manufacturing, tourism, and other tertiary activities. Some highland areas in Europe such as Switzerland and other parts of the Alps have already achieved these aims and no longer form problem regions. But most highland zones are still very far from success.

Two other types of economic region exist between these extremes. One is characterized by modernized farming, urban growth, and increasing employment opportunities in offices and factories. The outer parts of the Paris Basin provide an example of such areas, which can scarcely be called problem regions. By contrast, the final type of economic region did experience economic dynamism and urbanization in the past but has since lost its privileged position and now suffers from serious problems of social and economic maladjustment. Coalfields and old industrial areas, such as southern Belgium, northern France, and north-east England, are good examples of *maladjusted* regions which have lost the prosperity they once enjoyed when coal was the unrivalled source of industrial energy. Coal-mining throughout Europe has been rationalized since World War II because of competition from cheaper sources of energy such as hydro-electric power, oil, and natural gas. Far fewer miners are employed than in the past. In addition, the contraction of old-established manufacturing industries such as textiles, metallurgy, and ship-building has

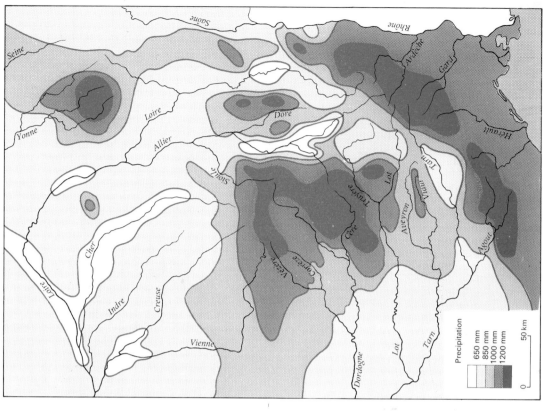

Fig. 2. Precipitation in the Massif Central

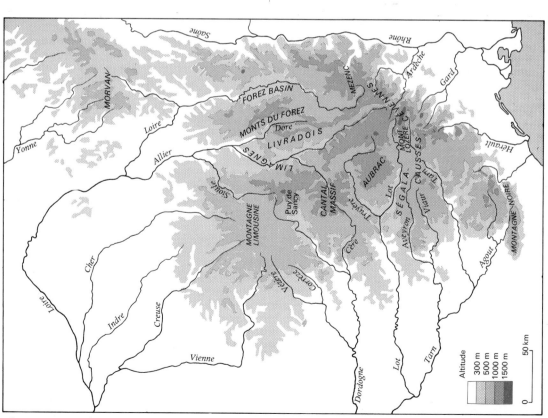

Fig. 1. Relief and sub-regions of the Massif Central

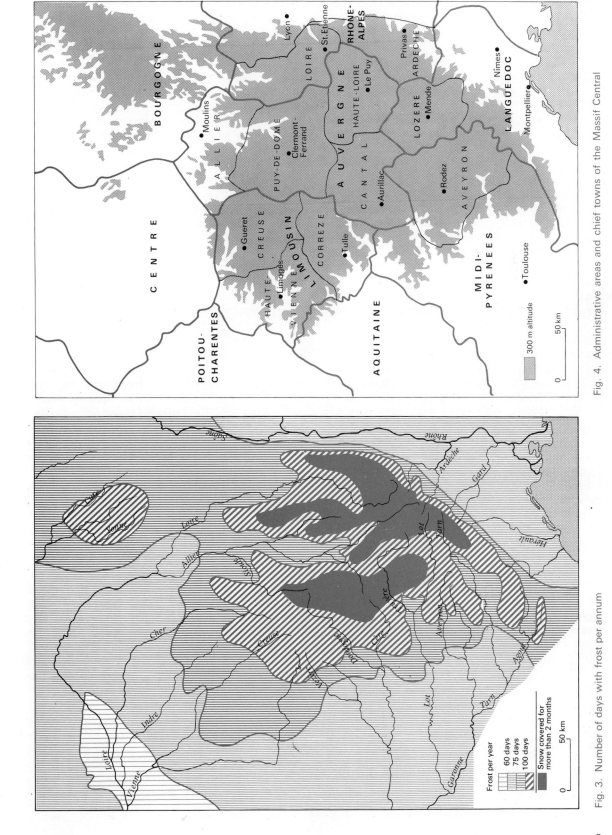

Fig. 4. Administrative areas and chief towns of the Massif Central

Fig. 3. Number of days with frost per annum

9

released large numbers of workers on to the labour market and has removed valuable sources of employment for young people. The maladjusted regions of Europe face the difficult tasks of attracting new jobs and renewing their drab urban environments which have been inherited from the industrial revolution.

The Massif Central: basis of the problem

The Massif Central is a roughly triangular upland area in central-southern France and covers one-sixth of the country. At first glance it appears to be the classic example of a *backward* region. The four main features which distinguish it from surrounding regions also suggest reasons for its present poverty.

1. It is highland terrain with a mean altitude of 1000 metres, but rising to 1886 metres in the Puy de Sancy (Fig. 1). The edge of the Massif Central is clearly defined in some areas, such as the mountain range of the Cévennes. But this is not always so and a gradual transition between mountain and plain exists in other areas. French geographers frequently use the 300-metre contour as a convenient boundary for the Massif. Their definition will be adopted in the following discussion.

2. Climatic conditions in the Massif are much harsher than in the surrounding lowlands. Precipitation is high, with more than 1200 mm per annum being recorded in the highest areas (Fig. 2). The whole of the Massif Central has more than 75 days of frost each year (Fig. 3) and in some parts only three months are frost-free. Large areas of ground are snow covered for more than two months each year, rising to six months in the high mountains. Snow patches remain in the cirques around the Puy de Sancy throughout most summers but there are no permanent ice-fields.

3. Soil conditions vary enormously from place to place within the Massif but they are much poorer than in the surrounding lowlands. The region has a very limited potential for successful arable farming.

4. The elevated and well-watered Massif Central forms a vast watershed from which rivers flow to the Mediterranean, Atlantic, and Channel coasts. These watercourses are not important for navigation but they provide routeways away from the mountain mass to other parts of France. In the nineteenth century, the geologist Elie de Beaumont described the Massif Central as the *pôle répulsif* of France; in other words, the region of dispersal from which rivers flowed, human beings migrated, and economic resources were dispatched to benefit other parts of the country.

Movement away from the Massif Central has always been more easy than movement into or through it.

These four features define the Massif Central as a region and partly suggest why it is recognized as a *problem region*. Its backwardness is all the more apparent when regional population characteristics and employment conditions are compared with those for the whole of France.

The total population of the eleven *départements* (Fig. 4) which correspond most closely to the area inside the 300-metre contour has decreased by 10 per cent from 3·81 millions in 1851 to 3·42 millions in 1975 (Table 1). Peak losses of 48 per cent were recorded in Lozère and Creuse *départements*. When the areas around the cities of Clermont-Ferrand, Limoges, and Saint-Etienne are excluded from the calculation, the population declined by 28 per cent. This is in very sharp contrast with the 47 per cent rise in the total French population over the same period.

For centuries young people with drive and initiative have migrated away from the harsh environment of the Massif Central in search of better jobs elsewhere in France. The region's remaining population is thus an aged one. Seventeen per cent of the Massif's inhabitants were aged over 65 in 1968 (Table 1). The national average was 13 per cent. By contrast only 30 per cent of the region's population was under 20, well below the national average of 32 per cent. But these figures are regional averages for the whole of the Massif. Some remote rural parts of the region are now almost totally devoid of young people.

The Massif is still predominantly agricultural and is peopled by country dwellers. Only 16 per cent of the French labour force was made up of people working on the land (farmers and labourers) in 1968 but in the Massif Central the proportion was double the national average (Table 1). Figures were very high in Aveyron (40 per cent), Cantal (45 per cent), Lozère (47 per cent) and Creuse (50 per cent) *départements*. Population densities in these mountainous farming regions are very low.

The agricultural systems of the Massif Central are inefficient by modern standards. Average cereal yields are only two-thirds the French average. This is not surprising in mountain country more suited to livestock farming than arable cultivation but even when stock rearing is included the Massif emerges as an impoverished farming region. The mean value per hectare of all farm produce (including livestock as well as crops) is only two-thirds of the French average and less than one-half of the figure for the Paris Basin.

TABLE 1

*Details of population and employment**

	Population (thousands)				Percentage Change:		Per-cent-age Urban	Density per sq. km.	Percentage working in:			Percentage of population aged:		
	1851	1962	1968	1975	1851–1975	1962–1975			Agri-culture	Indus-try	Terti-ary	Under 20	20–64	Over 64
Allier	336	380	387	378	+13	− 1	56	53	24	23	53	29	53	18
Ardeche	387	249	257	257	−34	+ 3	47	47	26	29	55	31	53	16
Aveyron	394	290	282	278	−29	− 4	39	32	40	18	42	29	54	17
Cantal	253	173	169	167	−34	− 3	29	29	45	11	44	32	53	15
Corrèze	320	238	238	241	−25	+ 1	41	41	36	19	45	28	54	18
Creuse	287	164	157	146	−49	−11	19	28	50	11	39	26	52	16
Haute-Loire	305	211	208	205	−33	− 3	41	42	38	24	38	31	51	18
Haute-Vienne	319	333	342	352	+10	+ 6	57	62	23	27	50	28	55	17
Loire	473	696	722	742	+57	+ 7	79	151	11	44	45	31	55	14
Lozère	145	82	77	75	−48	− 9	30	15	47	7	46	30	53	17
Puy-de-Dôme	597	509	548	581	− 3	+14	60	69	18	32	50	30	56	14
Massif Central	3816	3325	3387	3422	−10	+ 3	45	52	32	22	46	30	53	17
France	35 783	46 520	49 850	52 544	+47	+13	70	92	16	28	56	32	54	13

*1968 unless otherwise indicated

The agricultural labour force of the Massif Central is elderly as well as numerous. Seventy-two per cent of the region's farmers are over 50 years of age compared with 63 per cent nationally. Only 5 per cent are under 35, compared with 9 per cent for the whole of France. Elderly farmers tend to be backward-looking and unresponsive to change.

Some farms in the Massif are large but most holdings are small with 14 per cent under 5 ha, 74 per cent between 5 and 50 ha, and only 12 per cent over 50 ha (Table 2, p. 29).

Because of the continuing importance of farming, 55 per cent of the Massif's inhabitants lived in the countryside in 1968, almost twice the proportion for the whole of France (30 per cent). The region contains many small market towns, but few medium-sized towns and only three cities with more than 100 000 inhabitants. None of these acts as a regional centre for the whole of the Massif Central. Very great differences in the degree of urbanization exist between the various parts of the region. Only 45 per cent of the Massif's in-habitants were town dwellers in 1968 but in Loire and Puy-de-Dôme *départements* (containing Saint-Etienne and Clermont-Ferrand) the proportions rose to 79 per cent and 60 per cent.

For this reason it is not realistic to label the whole of the Massif Central as a *backward* type of problem region. This description certainly suits nine-tenths of the mountain mass but two other types of problem region are also found. *Mal-adjusted* regions are represented by industrial areas on the small coalfields of the Massif and by the many towns with historic craft industries. In addition, the area around Clermont-Ferrand forms a *dynamic* zone with important demo-graphic and economic growth.

The greatest problems facing planners in the Massif Central are to modernize farming and to diversify the whole of the rural economy by creat-ing new jobs in light manufacturing, services, and tourism. As a result, the region shares many com-mon problems with other upland areas of Europe such as Central Wales or the Highlands of Scotland.

2 Economic and Social Problems in the Massif Central

The past hundred years have witnessed large-scale urbanization throughout Europe. Population is concentrated around major administrative centres, along important routeways, at sites where coal is mined or raw materials provided for industrial processing. Such growth points, with the possible exception of mining areas, are rarely found in upland regions, which act as zones of dispersal. Because of their altitude, steep slopes, and harsh climate, movement in upland regions is more difficult than across surrounding lowlands or through major valleys. Important routeways avoid mountain zones wherever possible. Major administrative and trading centres are rarely found in highland terrain but the mining of coal

and metal ores and the development of manufacturing industry can stimulate important urban growth. This is illustrated by the cities of Saint-Etienne and Clermont-Ferrand in the Massif Central but they are exceptions to the general rule.

Industrial and urban growth has forged ahead in favoured localities beyond upland zones. Population has been attracted away from the poor environment of the mountains. Outmigration is a selective process, appealing to young people with initiative. The elderly and unambitious remain in their home communities and work the land. The types of farming that they practise are old-fashioned and more like the peasant ways of life

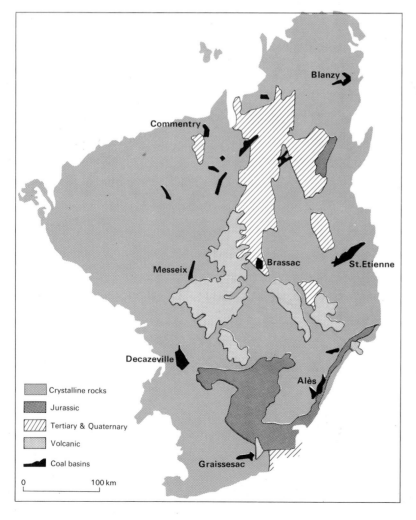

Fig. 5. Main geological divisions of the Massif Central

Blanzy

Commentry

Messeix   Brassac   St.Etienne

Decazeville

Alès

Crystalline rocks

Jurassic

Tertiary & Quaternary

Volcanic

Coal basins

0   100 km

Graissesac

that flourished before the railway age than the modern agricultural businesses which operate in lowland areas. The uplands of Europe still harbour too many aspects of economic life which have been only slightly modified since the breakdown of their traditional economies in the second half of the nineteenth century.

Traditional economies of the Massif Central

The traditional economies of the upland parts of Europe flourished before the railway age and supported large numbers of people at an almost subsistence level. Agricultural activities in each upland zone were far from uniform since peasant farmers adapted their ways of life to make use of the local resources presented by physical geography. Cereals were necessary for human subsistence and had to be grown throughout the upland areas before modern transportation allowed agricultural products to be brought in on a large scale but there were great local variations in the cereals that were actually produced.

Wheat was only grown in the most favoured parts of the Massif Central. These were the downfaulted troughs in the north of the Massif, crossed by the rivers Allier and Loire (Fig. 5). They contained the most fertile soils in the whole region and enjoyed a relatively dry and sunny climate in the lee of the Monts d'Auvergne. By contrast, buckwheat was grown on the plateaux of metamorphic and granitic rocks in the western section of the Massif where soils were base-poor, coarse, infertile, and often ill-drained. Damp and cloudy weather predominated, being brought by westerly winds that discharged their moisture as they rose over the mountain mass of the Auvergne. The physical environment of the Oceanic west was quite unsuited for wheat growing (Fig. 6). Rye formed the staple cereal crop elsewhere in the Massif. It was grown on the drier central and eastern plateaux and also in the dissected limestone country of the Causses which had suffered

Fig. 6. Types of climate in the Massif Central

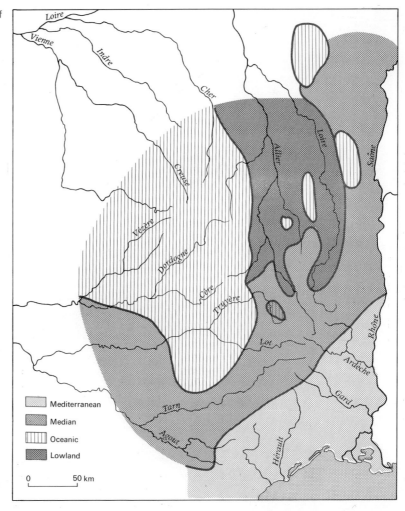

0   50 km

serious soil erosion after deforestation. The potato had been introduced to the Massif Central in the early nineteenth century and provided an important means of subsistence for large numbers of people. Similar types of peasant economy operated in pre-famine Ireland and in upland areas throughout Europe.

The basic peasant diet in the Massif Central consisted of rye bread, potato soup, and pig-meat. Sheep were reared for their wool which was used for cloth making and ewes' milk was made into cheese. Their manure was valuable for fertilizing arable fields. Cattle provided milk and meat and were important for pulling carts and farm implements. Chestnuts were grown below 600 metres in the southern parts of the Massif with a Mediterranean type of climate. They formed a valuable multi-purpose crop which could be dried and milled into flour for human consumption and also provided fodder for livestock. Their timber was used for building and for firewood. Five different types of farming region were found in the Massif Central in the early nineteenth century (Fig. 7). They corresponded closely to local variations in soil, climate, and relief.

1. Mixed farming with wheat growing took place on the fertile soils of the northern troughs (Limagnes) which supported high densities of population living in large, nucleated villages. Ploughland was fragmented into an enormous number of tiny plots. Farming had previously been organized on a communal basis with fallow land being grazed by communal flocks of sheep.

2. A completely different type of farming was practised in northern and western parts of the Massif Central, from the Morvan to the Montagne Noire. The humid oceanic climate was not suited to cereal growing and only that which was absolutely necessary for subsistence was produced. The environment was far more favourable for cattle rearing. Pastures were surrounded by hedges in an enclosed landscape (bocage) with

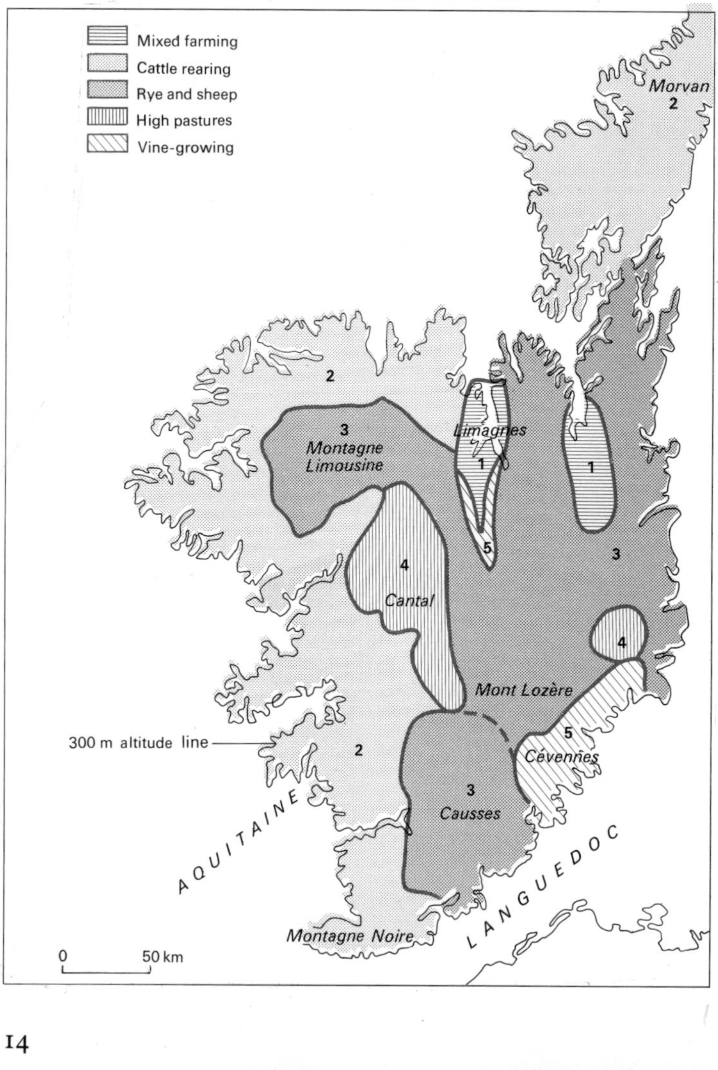

Fig. 7. Agricultural regions of the Massif Central

Mixed farming
Cattle rearing
Rye and sheep
High pastures
Vine-growing

Morvan
2

2

3
Montagne
Limousine

Limagnes
1

1

5

3

4

Cantal

4

Mont Lozère

5

Cévennes

300 m altitude line

2

3
Causses

AQUITAINE

LANGUEDOC

Montagne Noire

0   50 km

In the heyday of the traditional rural economy of the Massif Central, trackways (*drailles*) between permanent pastures and improved fields were used for herding transhumant sheep between the lowlands of Languedoc and the summer pastures of mountain areas in the southern parts of the Massif

small hamlets which contrasted with the open fields and large nucleated villages of the Limagnes.

3. The agricultural system of the remainder of the high plateaux and the limestone Causses involved growing rye and rearing sheep for wool and meat. Livestock grazed communal moorland (*landes*) in uplands from the Montagne Limousine to Mont Lozère. Small parts of the *landes* were cleared by burning and were cultivated for a few years to supplement permanent crop production around the small hamlets.

4. Even rye cultivation was virtually impossible in the very high volcanic areas of the Massif with their harsh climatic conditions. Grass grew abundantly in such damp areas above the margins of permanent settlement. The high pastures (known as *montagnes*) were only used on a seasonal basis for transhumance. Cattle were taken there from farms in lower areas for grazing throughout the summer. Stockmen lived in stone-built shelters (*burons*) and made cheese which was sold so that cereals could be bought for human consumption.

5. The final type of farming involved vine-growing. This was restricted to very small parts of the Massif Central, such as the sheltered hillslopes bordering the lowland troughs of the Limagnes and the sunny, almost Mediterranean hillslopes of the Cévennes. Land was fragmented into tiny plots and was often terraced. Very high densities of population were supported by this intensive agricultural activity.

The goods and livestock produced in each of these agricultural regions had to be exchanged for products from other parts of the Massif Central and from nearby regions beyond its borders. Many small towns with weekly markets and seasonal livestock fairs flourished at points of contact between contrasting agricultural regions. A ring of small towns developed around the high pastures of the Cantal for the sale of cheese and livestock. Other towns in contact zones had markets for the exchange of local goods with products from Aquitaine, Languedoc, and other surrounding regions. The northern troughs (Limagnes) which penetrated the mountain zone and formed the only important natural routeway into the Massif contained important market centres such as Riom and Clermont-Ferrand.

Many farmers and farmworkers in upland parts of Europe could not survive on the meagre profits of farming and had to take on a variety of supplementary jobs which provided additional incomes. Agriculture was combined with seasonal fishing in coastal areas of Scotland, Ireland, Norway, and elsewhere. In central and northern Europe part-time forestry work provided a means of obtaining additional incomes. Other solutions had to be found in the land-locked Massif Central. Farming families worked at many craft activities in winter when agricultural work was slack because of bad weather. Cloth-producing towns, such as Nîmes and Montpellier (Fig. 4), sited beyond the

Haymaking in the high pastoral areas of the Massif Central in Puy-de-Dôme

margins of the Massif Central, employed out-workers in southern parts of the highland zone. Many villages in the eastern part of the Massif housed lacemakers who dispatched their goods to Le Puy, Saint-Etienne, and Lyon. Elsewhere in the Massif the agricultural population spent part of the winter making small goods such as nails and farm implements from wood, leather, metal, and other materials.

In addition to these domestic crafts, carried on in the farmers' own homes, numerous workshop industries flourished and provided work and additional incomes for members of farming families. Small workshops producing woollen cloths, paper, light metal goods, glass, and other products lined the banks of swift-flowing streams that tumbled from the mountains to valleys and plains and provided the necessary motive power for rudimentary machinery. Variations on this kind of dual economy, combining agriculture with industry, were found in many parts of upland Europe.

Outworking and workshop crafts were not available in all parts of upland Europe. In the Alps and the Pyrenees as well as in some parts of the Massif Central seasonal migration was necessary to obtain supplementary incomes. One type of migration simply involved farmworkers moving to different agricultural regions to help farmers at harvest time and other busy periods of the farming year when extra labour was needed. In the Massif Central farm labourers often moved from their home villages for a few weeks each year to harvest wheat in the Limagnes, cut hay in the high pastoral areas, or help with the grape harvest in the Cévennes.

Another form of temporary migration involved farm workers moving to jobs outside their home region in winter. Labourers from the Massif Central worked as treefellers in Lorraine or as harvesters in Aquitaine and Languedoc. Others took non-agricultural jobs and travelled to Paris, Lyon, and even to Spain, as tinkers and sellers of cloth, wine, firewood, and many other wares. The best known seasonal migration involved the movement of labourers from Limousin to work as builders in Paris and Lyon. But it was unusual, taking place in the summer months because building work was only possible in fine weather. Much farm work in Limousin was left to womenfolk and old people. Sometimes extra labourers had to be brought in from other parts of the Massif.

Craftwork and seasonal migration were important in the traditional rural economies of upland parts of Europe for two main reasons. First, they were essential to supplement local agricultural resources which were insufficient to support the large numbers of people who lived in the countryside. Second, they provided upland dwellers with contacts in surrounding regions. These family links were to prove extremely important when the traditional economies broke down during the nineteenth century and permanent outmigration took place on a massive scale.

Breakdown of the traditional economies

The mediocre resources of upland parts of Europe were being stretched to the limit to support large numbers of people in the first half of the nineteenth century. Birth rates were very high in the Massif Central and population pressure pushed the upper limits of cultivation into mountain areas with poor soils and harsh climatic conditions where crop yields were very low. Serious rural poverty threatened if harvests of subsistence crops such as rye, potatoes, and chestnuts were to fail because of consistently bad weather.

This took place during the 1840s in the Massif Central, Ireland, and other parts of Europe when a run of harsh summers produced very poor harvests of rye and potatoes. The old agricultural systems of these areas were severely disrupted. Famine occurred and the inhabitants' resistance to disease was lowered. Adult death rates soared and infantile mortality was extremely high. Outmigration encouraged by rural poverty combined with a temporary excess of deaths over births to produce serious depopulation. Subsistence crops in the Massif Central also failed later in the century. But these failures were on a smaller scale and affected parts of the region rather than the whole Massif. Other crops in addition to rye and potatoes were also very vulnerable. In the closing decades of the nineteenth century the vines of the Cévennes and the Limagnes, which had supported large numbers of people, were destroyed by vine-root disease (*phylloxera*). The old agricultural systems of the Massif were wrecked beyond hope of repair. Outmigration to the towns of the Limagnes and more especially to other parts of France formed the only means of escape from intense rural poverty.

Craft industries which had flourished prior to the mid-nineteenth century and had supported the precarious rural economies of upland regions also underwent serious decline. They had to face severe competition from cheap, factory-produced goods from rapidly industrializing areas around major cities, coal basins, and seaports. At the same time local demands for craft goods contracted as depopulation reduced the total number of people living in the countryside.

In the final decades of the nineteenth century and early years of the twentieth century improvements in transportation in upland regions brought factory goods and farm products from other parts of Europe into direct competition with local products for the first time. The mountain environment of the Massif Central made the construction of railways and roads a slow and costly business. Deep gorges, incised into the plateau surfaces, restricted movement and raised building costs enormously since long viaducts had to be constructed across valleys such as the Sioule and the Truyère (Fig. 8). Steep slopes slowed down movement both by road and rail. A skeleton network of railway lines had been constructed in the Massif by the early years of the present century, though some of these were intended primarily to link areas outside the Massif rather than to serve the upland area itself.

The easiest journey between two points is rarely achieved by a straight line in this mountainous terrain and railways pursue tortuous routes in an attempt to avoid gorges and to minimize gradients. This is particularly true for lines which cut across the natural 'grain' of the country, such as the route between Limoges and Clermont-Ferrand which skirts round the highest parts of the Monts d'Auvergne. Even in good weather conditions many trains require two locomotives to negotiate steep gradients. Heavy snowfall interrupts services in winter and icy conditions make road journeys hazardous. It is not surprising that

French Government Tourist Office
The Garabit viaduct, constructed between 1882 and 1884

the main roads and railway lines between Paris and South-west France or the Mediterranean coast avoid the Massif Central.

The construction of road and rail networks reduced the isolation of the upland regions of Europe and partially integrated them into their respective national economies. As a result, the weaknesses of traditional craft and agricultural activities were shown up and the inefficient economies of the uplands declined even further. The construction of roads and railways made great demands on local supplies of agricultural labour. Navvies moved away from their home villages when they were laying the railway tracks. Once these had been completed an easy and relatively cheap means of travel was available for country dwellers to migrate to find more attractive and better paid jobs in the cities.

Rural depopulation

All the factors which disrupted traditional economic life in the uplands also accelerated their depopulation. It is very difficult to distinguish between cause and effect in the complicated syndrome of rural decline and despair. After population growth in the first half of the nineteenth century, the Massif Central entered a long period of decline which continues to the present day.

Depopulation has not taken place at a constant rate. A strong wave of outmigration occurred in the 1840s. This was a flight from poverty and involved day labourers, unemployed craftsmen, and small farmers. In spite of this dramatic loss, birth rates remained high and the severity of

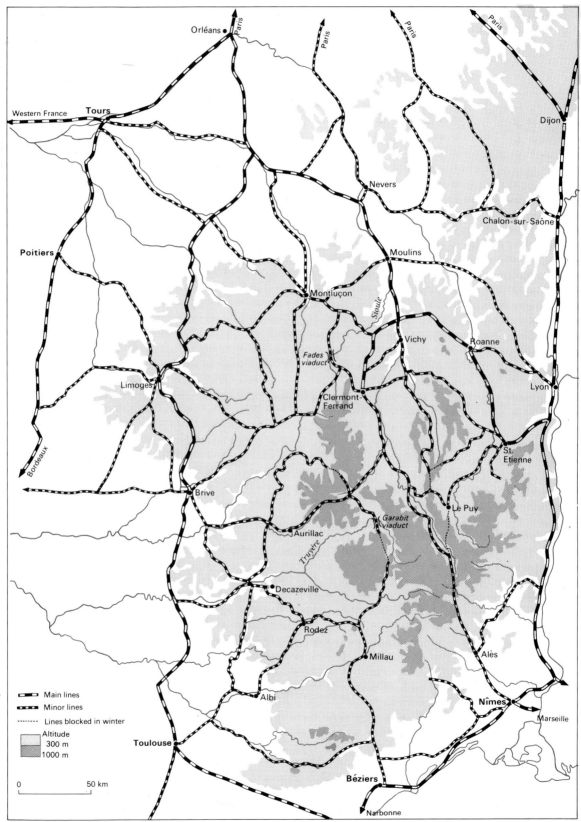

Fig. 8. Railways in the Massif Central

out-migration was concealed. Ardèche, Cantal, Lozère, and Puy-de-Dôme *départements* had reached their population maxima by 1851 (Table 1) but peak figures were not recorded in other areas until later in the century (Fig. 9). Out-migration was very strong from all parts of the Massif after 1880. In some areas this combined with natural decrease and produced a very grave demographic situation.

Other factors, which were by no means unique to the Massif Central, speeded up outmigration in the closing years of the century. Railway construction required labour and provided opportunities for further outmigration. Coal-mining centres (Alès, Decazeville, Saint-Etienne) and industrial towns (Limoges) were growing rapidly and required labour which was supplied by migrants from the countryside. Loire and Haute-Vienne *départements*, containing the cities of Saint-Etienne and Limoges, experienced population growth throughout the 19th century (Fig. 9). The expansion of Paris, Lyon, and other major cities demanded armies of building workers which were provided by less-developed parts of France, including the Massif Central. The well-established seasonal movements of people from upland areas in search of work in other parts of France were replaced by permanent outmigration.

The specialized economies of the Limagnes and the Cévennes were ruined by diseases affecting the vines and silkworms in the closing decades of the century. The agricultural crises which followed intensified depopulation. The gradual spread of primary education in village schools taught farm children about the attractions of city life. Similarly, military service took young men away from their home villages and stationed them in barracks close to urban areas. All these processes worked together to intensify outmigration. Large numbers of young and middle-aged men were killed during World War I. The pattern of marriages and births in the Massif Central (and in other parts of France) was severely disrupted, not only in wartime but also in the next two

Fig. 9. Population changes in the Massif Central 1801–1968 (by *département*)

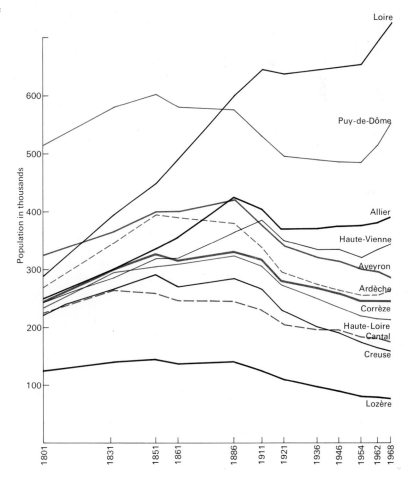

decades since heads of families and marriage partners had been killed off. The population of each *département* in the Massif fell rapidly between 1911 and 1921 (Fig. 9). The results were particularly disastrous in the countryside, which did not benefit from inmigration.

The whole of the Massif Central lost 10 per cent of its population between 1851 and 1975 (Table 1). The smallness of this figure is due to the fact that some large urban areas continued to grow throughout the period and thereby concealed serious losses that took place in the countryside. Between 1901 and 1954 the Massif lost 17 per cent of its inhabitants, far more than any other backward area of France, such as the Pyrenees (6 per cent) or Aquitaine (14 per cent). Losses of over 40 per cent were recorded in country areas in high Limousin and in the mountain spine running from Thiers in the north to the Cévennes in the south (Fig. 10). Many villages and small towns in eastern parts of the Massif, which had been supported by a combination of farming and craft activities, lost

between two-thirds and three-quarters of their population in half a century.

In spite of this general pattern of decline, population growth took place around coalfields, traditional industrial centres and towns in the Massif Central. Three phases of population growth may be recognized. The first involved dispersed workshop activities which flourished during much of the nineteenth century. The second involved the rise of coal-mining and metallurgical industries in the hey-day of the coal-based, steam-powered industrial revolution. Both of these types of manufacturing have experienced serious contraction in the present century and have given rise to the *maladjusted* areas of the Massif Central. The third phase of growth involved many types of industry which have been installed in the northern parts of the Massif, largely since 1900 in response to the following factors: the region's strategic importance, being far from vulnerable frontiers; adequate supplies of labour; good communications with Paris; energy supplies from

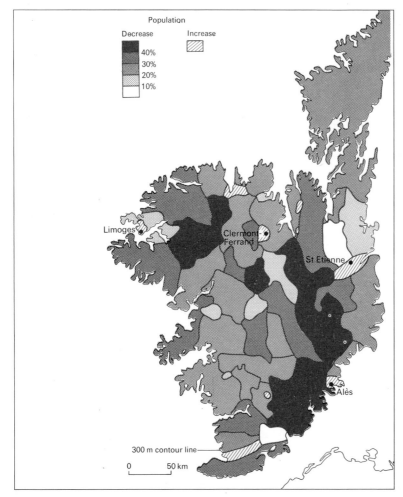

Fig. 10. Population changes in the Massif Central between 1901 and 1954

hydro-electric power; and, more recently, the Government's policy for stimulating manufacturing in relatively under-developed parts of France. The concentration of new industries in the Limagnes has given rise to the only really *dynamic* area in the Massif Central.

Maladjusted areas:
the decline of workshop industries

Surviving workshop industries retain much of their old craft organization and have not been fully mechanized. Their products are of a high quality but are expensive. They are highly vulnerable to competition from mass-produced articles from other parts of France and from abroad. Three examples serve to illustrate problems which face the workshop trades.

The glove industry of **Millau** rose to importance in the mid-eighteenth century using the skins of young lambs born in the nearby Causses. Workshop activities in the town were complemented by outworking in villages up to 50 km from Millau where skins were distributed for making up into gloves. Since World War II extra emphasis has been placed on outworking in an attempt to keep wages and general production costs as low as possible. But the industry is threatened in four main ways. The hinterland of Millau is losing population rapidly and labour for outworking is disappearing. Mechanized glove producers in France and elsewhere can produce gloves far more cheaply. In addition, they can use a variety of fabrics and can change colours and designs to follow, or indeed to create, fashions. By contrast, the glove industry of Millau is expensive, organized in an old-fashioned way, and is highly vulnerable to changes in glove fashion.

The growth of **Limoges** during the nineteenth century was due to the rise of the porcelain industry which made use of local sources of kaolin. The industry was in the hands of family firms which produced high-quality but expensive tableware and exported large quantities to Germany, Italy, Spain, and the U.S.A. With this apparently firm industrial base, as well as its role as a regional centre, the city's population rose from 51 000 in 1861 to 84 000 in 1901 when Limoges was far larger than Clermont-Ferrand (53 000). Unfortunately the porcelain industry has not flourished in the present century. Overseas markets have been lost to cheaper producers in Japan, Germany and Czechoslovakia. Old-established family firms were unable to raise sufficient capital to modernize their industry. Neither could they adapt production to meet new demands. The industry

French Government Tourist Office

Electrical energy has replaced water power as the motive force in scores of small workshops producing cutlery along the banks of the swift-flowing river Durolle at Thiers

declined and its labour force fell from 10 000 in 1901 to 2500 in the early 1960s. This affected the whole of the city, which entered half a century of economic stagnation.

The cutlery trade of **Thiers** provides another variation on the problems of workshop industries. It flourished from the medieval period onwards as craftsmen produced many types of cutting tool in workshops that lined the banks of the Durolle river where it descended from the Forez upland to the Limagnes and provided power for rudimentary machinery. In addition, a complex system of outworking operated in nearby villages with farmers combining agricultural work in summer with cutlery making in winter. The industry remained at the workshop stage with very complicated forms of sub-contracting between different craftsmen. Such an antiquated arrangement could not stand up to competition from cheap, factory-produced cutlery in the present century. The industry was cushioned from overseas competitors during World War II but since then cheap, foreign-produced cutlery has captured markets in France and in her former colonies. Thiers still produces two-thirds of all French cutlery but the industry is divided between a large number of small firms. Only eight employ more than fifty workers apiece. The remaining 4000 workshop craftsmen and 1500 outworkers are employed in 400 small concerns.

Maladjusted areas:
the problems of coal-based industrial areas

The coalfields of the Massif Central are the region's most seriously *maladjusted* areas. The coal industry has greatly reduced its workforce since World War II and manufacturing industries located on the coalfields are also shedding labour. Coal Measures are found in a number of small, faulted basins in the Massif which have played an important part in the history of French industrialization (Fig. 5). Unfortunately, the coal seams are thin, fractured, and mixed with bands of sterile material. Mining is very costly when compared with highly mechanized extraction, for example, in Lorraine.

The industrial revolution in France started in these small coal basins where coke replaced charcoal for smelting local iron ores. In 1785 the first 'English style' blast furnace was built at Le Creusot and for a while this was the leading iron-making area in France. This situation did not last long and coke-fired blast furnaces were set up in the early nineteenth century on rival coalfields at Saint-Etienne, Decazeville, and Alès. New forms of communication were constructed in these mining and industrial areas. The first French railway was built westwards from Saint-Etienne to the river Loire in 1828 and the second eastwards to Lyon four years later. By the mid-nineteenth century the coal basins of Saint-Etienne, Blanzy, Decazeville, Alès, and Commentry had become important industrial and urban centres. Other coal basins in the Massif Central developed only small mining communities in the midst of the countryside. In 1850 one-third of all French coal was mined at Saint-Etienne. This was well ahead of the Northern coalfield which provided only one-fifth at that time.

The pre-eminence of the coal-based industrial areas of the Massif Central did not last long. Local deposits of iron ore were exhausted. Ores had to be brought in from other parts of France. The rise of efficient metallurgical centres in northern France was to the detriment of producers in the Massif. Their importance was further reduced after 1880 following the application of the Gilchrist–Thomas process which allowed the phosphoric *minette* ores of Lorraine to be used in steelmaking. In order to consolidate their position, metallurgical firms in the Massif turned increasingly to the production of high quality steels and engineering goods. Thus, for example, the broad-based metallurgical industry of Le Creusot was reorganized to produce special steels for locomotives and to manufacture arms.

Old industrial areas in the Massif Central have continued to decrease in importance in the face of competition from more efficient producers in northern and north-eastern France. Only during wartime have the industries of the Massif been temporarily boosted when mining and manufacturing areas in northern France have been occupied by the enemy or have been under heavy attack. Changes in national frontiers as a result of French military defeat in the Franco–Prussian War were also to the advantage of the Massif Central. The cotton textile industry in Roanne and nearby towns on the eastern edge of the Massif was stimulated when the cotton-manufacturing areas of Alsace were occupied by Germany between 1871 and World War I. The mines and factories of central France flourished in postwar recovery periods but their weaknesses became all too clear once the industries of northern France started to function properly again.

The problems of the mining areas of the Massif Central have become increasingly grave since 1945. Some small coal basins have been worked out. The others are very expensive sources of energy when compared with coal from Lorraine or from abroad, imported oil, and natural gas from Lacq in south-west France which is now piped to the coalfield towns of Decazeville, Montluçon/Commentry, Saint-Etienne, and Le Creusot. In the early 1960s losses were made on every ton of coal mined in the Massif, varying from 50 francs at Saint-Etienne, 35 at Alès, 20 at Decazeville and the small basins of the Auvergne, to 12 francs at Blanzy. One-half of the French coal industry's total deficit resulted from the inefficiency of these small basins.

A national plan for running down coal production in France was announced in 1960. Production from the Centre-Midi basins (roughly corresponding to the Massif Central) was to be cut from 14·3 million tons in 1950 to 11·4 million tons in 1965. In the intervening years 6000 colliery workers were to be released from the mines of the Centre-Midi by implementing early retirement, not recruiting new men, and directing miners to jobs in the Northern and Lorraine coalfields.

This initial phase of rationalization caused great unrest in the colliery towns of the Massif, and especially at Decazeville. In 1960 the Government announced that the town's mines would be closed in 1965 and the great opencast pit of La Découverte a few years later. This was seen as a 'death warrant' by the local miners. They protested that productivity per manshift had doubled in the previous decade and that reserves of coal still remained to be worked. They feared that their living standards would fall if they had to move to other mining areas or take on alternative jobs in local factories which had not yet been established. The miners considered that coal-mining should be run down gradually in the period up to 1975 to allow adequate time for new jobs to be created. To demonstrate their concern they went on strike in the mine shafts for 64 days at the end of 1961. Passionate public interest was aroused throughout France. The decision to close the mines in 1965 was not revoked but the Government assured the miners that every effort would be made to open new factories. The workforce was run down by several hundred men each year between 1960 and 1965, in contrast with the earlier figure of 50 retirements annually. Miners were pensioned off early, dismissed, or encouraged to move to other mining areas. Coal-mining has now ceased completely. New industries have been brought to Decazeville but some firms were financially unstable and have closed their factories after only a short time. Ex-miners who moved to jobs in other areas have found more security than those who remained at Decazeville.

In 1968 an even more serious decision was taken regarding the future of coal-mining in the Massif Central. Production would be stopped at Saint-Etienne in 1973. Two years later the pits at Alès and in the three remaining mining areas of the Auvergne (Brassac, Messeix, and Saint-Eloy) would be closed. Only the mines at Blanzy and Carmaux which supply large thermal power stations were reprieved. As a result of this decision, the mining areas of the Massif Central face enormous problems of economic and social readjustment. Finding jobs to replace those which have been lost is difficult enough, but in addition the whole environment of nineteenth century housing, tip heaps and dereliction needs to be tidied up or cleared away so that industrialists may be attracted to open new factories and local inhabitants may regain the confidence they have lost in the future of their home area.

Dynamic areas and new sources of power

By contrast with the stagnation of workshop trades, coal-mining, and old manufacturing activities, important industrial growth has taken place in some parts of the Massif Central during the present century. Rubber manufacturing at Clermont-Ferrand provides the best example and is the key activity from which the whole of the city's recent expansion has stemmed. Hydro-electric power has provided the Massif with a new source of energy but this has been to the advantage of other parts of France as much as to the region itself. Recent growth in population and

Coal extraction now continues in only two of the many mining areas in the Massif Central and on its margins. The great open-cast pit of La Découverte at Decazeville provides a striking example of the impact of coal-mining in a predominantly rural region

industrial activity has benefited only a small area in the north of the Massif. Few factories have been opened elsewhere.

The initial establishment of the rubber industry at Clermont-Ferrand owed nothing to the geography of the surrounding area. It depended entirely on the initiative of two Parisian entrepreneurs, Messieurs Barbier and Daubrée, who had family connexions with Clermont-Ferrand. In the early 1820s they had tried to start a factory for extracting sugar from beet grown in the Limagnes. Their scheme failed and in 1828 they opened a factory for manufacturing rubber, largely because of their contacts with the Scots industrialist Mackintosh, who was the uncle of Madame Daubrée. In the 1830s one hundred workers were employed in the rubber industry which formed only a small component in the employment pattern of Clermont-Ferrand.

Really rapid growth came after the Michelin family took over the firm in 1899. The workforce increased from 500 in 1901 to 3600 in 1911 and 19 000 in 1921. Such a rapid rise resulted from a combination of factors which benefited Clermont-Ferrand. The national need for rubber during World War I (over and above the growing demands of the youthful motor-car industry) meant that the Government was keen to expand factories which already produced tyres and other rubber products. Clermont-Ferrand was in a 'safe' location far from the vulnerable Northern and North-eastern frontiers which were open to attack from Germany. Hydro-electric power was available from recent schemes in the Massif. Vineyard areas in the Limagnes, the rural economy of which had been ruined by vine-root disease, provided a suitable labour force. In addition, the city of Clermont-Ferrand was in easy communication with Paris by road and rail for receiving raw materials and dispatching finished products.

The continued growth of rubber manufacturing has formed the basis of the expansion of Clermont-Ferrand. Now the industry has more than 25 000 employees. Half of them are actually involved in manufacturing and the remainder work in the corporation's offices, dispatch services, and ancillary activities. The Michelin firm has created a 'city within a city' making Clermont-Ferrand the classic example of a 'company town'. Manufacturing and office activities are located at five large sites, ranging from the oldest at Les Carmes close to the city centre, to Ladoux (near Riom) where modern research installations are located (Fig. 11). Michelin has constructed large numbers of flats and houses for its employees on housing estates (cités Michelin) of varying dates

and styles. The corporation also operates special Michelin schools, grocery shops, clinics, and sports stadia for the benefit of its employees and their families.

Since 1945 Michelin has not constructed its own housing but has relied on the large estates built by the city administration. In addition, many workers of predominantly rural origin commute long distances by car or company bus from surrounding villages. In 1963 5000 workers on the Michelin payroll lived between 5 km and 20 km from their place of work and a further 1000 lived more than 20 km away. Many are 'worker-peasants' (ouvriers-paysans) who live on the small farms they have inherited around Clermont-Ferrand. These holdings are worked in the evenings and at weekends with help from members of the owner's family. The rubber industry of Clermont-Ferrand is incomparable in size and importance with any other manufacturing activity in the Massif Central. Not only has it accounted for the phenomenal growth of the Clermont-Ferrand urban area (53 000 inhabitants in 1901; 250 000 in 1975) but its commuting labour force helps integrate villages from Gannat in the north

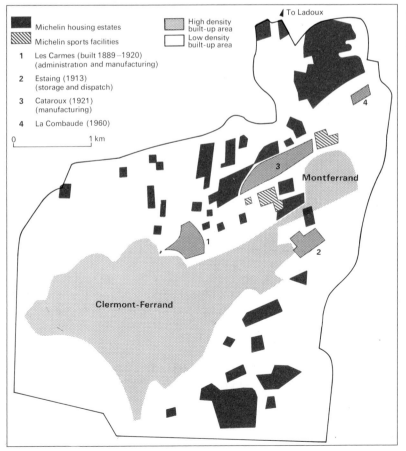

Michelin housing estates
Michelin sports facilities

High density built-up area
Low density built-up area

1 Les Carmes (built 1889–1920) (administration and manufacturing)

2 Estaing (1913) (storage and dispatch)

3 Cataroux (1921) (manufacturing)

4 La Combaude (1960)

0   1 km

To Ladoux

Montferrand

Clermont-Ferrand

Fig. 11. The place of the Michelin Corporation in the townscape of Clermont-Ferrand

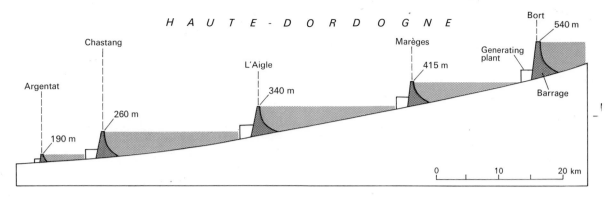

Fig. 12. Hydro-electric installations in the upper valley of the Dordogne

to Brassac in the south into a large and increasingly congested urbanized area.

The development of hydro-electric power since 1910 introduced a new source of energy to the Massif Central and permitted further industrialization. The main rivers of the region rise in areas with over 1200 mm of precipitation each year. River flow is often slight in summer and dams have had to be built across gorge-like valleys to create reservoirs, which to a certain extent even out the flow of water for electricity generation throughout the year. The national grid now allows the winter precipitation maxima in the Massif Central to fit conveniently into the national pattern of hydro-electric power generation and to complement the summer maxima of the Alps and Pyrenees.

Small hydro-electric power schemes were started on the Sioule and Dordogne rivers before World War I and permitted the rapid growth of the rubber industry. The first large scheme was on the Truyère river in the 1930s. Since 1945 the Creuse, Dordogne, Tarn, and their headwaters have been converted into 'staircases of water' with flights of barrages and generating stations alternating with reservoirs (Fig. 12). The highest dam and the largest reservoir (24 km long and up to 4 km wide) is on the Dordogne at Bort-les-Orgues. In addition to generating massive quantities of power, this scheme regulates the flow of water to other stations downstream. At present between one-fifth and one-quarter of French hydro-electric power is generated in the Massif Central. Half of this total is used by domestic and industrial consumers in the region. The remainder is fed into the national grid for transmission to Paris and other cities or is consumed by the railway network.

Hydro-electric power generation has not led to widespread industrialization in the Massif Central. However the availability of power has been one of the contributory factors favouring industrial growth since 1910. In addition to the rubber industry, other examples include the steelworks at Les Ancizes, west of Clermont-Ferrand (using hydro-electric power from the Sioule valley) and at Saint-Chély-d'Apcher in the Truyère valley. The installation of factories to produce electrical signals and cables at Riom depended on contacts with the central Government in Paris, but they also used hydro-electric power from the Sioule valley. In the 1930s policies were implemented for decentralizing strategic industries from Paris and northern and north-eastern France. Issoire was selected as a suitable site for an aluminium rolling mill which now employs 1600 workers. The availability of hydro-electric power from the Dordogne played no small part in this decision. The same factors were of importance when works producing aero-engines were moved to Riom.

The transmission of electric energy in the twentieth century has introduced a flexibility of industrial location which was unthinkable in the age of water power or coal. Most new and dynamic industries have been installed in or around the lowland trough of the Limagnes. Traditional industries have also been supplied with hydro-electric power but few new factories have been opened in the mountain zone. Industrial implantation to diversify the economy of the upland parts of the Massif Central is just one of the tasks facing regional planners.

25

3 Planning the Massif Central: The Countryside

Little action was taken by French Governments before World War II to tackle the various social and economic problems which had developed in the provinces. It is true that the Government had authorized the expansion of key provincial industries during World War I and in the 1920s and 1930s but this had been done for strategic reasons rather than to help the provinces and diversify their economies. Since World War II a very complex system of planning has developed in France to cover virtually all aspects of social and economic life. In addition to a series of national plans, programmes for regional improvement have been drawn up for each of the country's twenty-one official planning areas.

The Massif Central is covered by six of these (Fig. 4). Northern and central parts of the region form the Auvergne and Limousin planning areas, centred on Clermont-Ferrand and Limoges. The remainder of the Massif is divided between Rhône-Alpes (Lyon), Languedoc (Montpellier), Midi-Pyrénées (Toulouse), and Bourgogne (Dijon). This situation reflects the fragmentation of other upland areas in Europe, such as the Pennines, between a number of administrative units directed from outside. The economic and social problems of the Massif Central have not been investigated comprehensively, nor have planning proposals been submitted for the whole of the mountain mass. The problems of those parts of the Massif administered from beyond its borders have been dismissed as being of marginal importance to the general development of Languedoc, Midi-Pyrénées, and Rhône-Alpes. Even the special regional divisions used for implementing the proposals of the Sixth National Plan (1971-5) failed to treat the Massif as a single unit and divided it four ways between the South-west, Mediterranean France, the Lyon Region, and the Paris Basin. For purposes of simplicity the following discussion will not dwell on the social and administrative fragmentation of the Massif. It must not be forgotten, however, that this prevents it being managed in an integrated fashion as a single problem region.

Planning the countryside

The Massif Central has the unhappy distinction of containing some of the most backward parts of Western Europe. The natural environment is poor but the real problems of agricultural backwardness in the Massif, and in other upland parts of Europe, arise from a failure to use the land efficiently to yield crops and livestock products which are in current demand and will guarantee a reasonable standard of living for the farming population. All too often upland farmers in Europe continue to manage their land in a way reminiscent of the traditional agricultural systems which operated before the railway age. Many of them view farming as a way of life rather than as an economic activity which demands efficient production and marketing.

The pressure of farming population on limited land resources has greatly decreased in Europe over the past hundred years and, as a result, almost 'automatic' changes in agricultural activity have taken place. Nevertheless, many other features have been inherited from the past and survive in a virtually unmodified form. A few examples will show the kind of problems that are faced not only in the Massif Central but elsewhere in Europe.

In the past, arable land was fragmented into tiny plots for working by hand or with very simple implements at a time when the agricultural population was far more numerous than today. In regions where communal systems of peasant farming had once operated the plots held by each individual owner were scattered widely throughout the village's farmland so that he and his neighbours each had access to soils of differing quality. Systems of communal farming have now disappeared and the agricultural population is far smaller than in the past. Nevertheless, the tiny scattered plots remain in many parts of Western and Central Europe and form a major hindrance to attempts to modernize, and especially to mechanize, farming. Enclosure and land consolidation in past centuries swept away the tiny plots in Great Britain and Scandinavia and replaced them by large fields. This task still has to be done in much of Western Europe, including the Massif Central.

Many of the farms in Western Europe are far too small to be efficient in an age of mechanization. Similarly the settlement pattern of rural areas is too dispersed and the total population living in individual settlements too small for each village and hamlet to continue to support its own

This valley in the Cévennes has experienced serious depopulation in the last hundred years. Many terraces, once used for vine-growing, have been abandoned and invaded by trees and scrub. Agricultural activities now cluster on the lower slopes and along the road in the valley floor

primary school, shops, and other services that country dwellers have come to expect from their exposure to TV, radio, and other mass media.

Whole systems of land use in upland areas have been inherited from the past but are no longer viable in the modern world. Two examples from the Massif Central will illustrate the kind of problem involved. The steep hillslopes of the Cévennes and the borders of the Limagnes flourished as terraced vineyards until the late nineteenth century. Land was divided into extremely tiny plots and supported very high densities of population. Since the scourge of vine-root disease the hillslopes have been abandoned to scrub. Neighbouring villages have become severely depopulated. A far more serious land use problem exists on the high granitic plateaux of the Massif which were formerly used for grazing communal flocks of sheep and the cultivation of temporary crops of rye. This type of economy no longer survives and large areas of land have fallen completely out of agricultural use and have reverted to woodland or scrub.

Examples of this kind could be multiplied from many other upland areas. In Eastern Europe radical measures such as land reform and agricultural collectivization have been used to sweep away old patterns of farms, fields, and land use and to replan them for modern farming. Such an approach is not desirable in the political climate of Western Europe, but individual governments have employed gentler and more gradual methods in an attempt to transform agricultural activities and to modernize rural life.

In 1968 Dr. Sicco Mansholt presented a hard-hitting report on farming in the Common Market countries and went on to suggest measures to rescue it from being an antiquated, tradition-bound way of life. The agricultural labour force was too large and ill-educated. Farms were too small. Too much land was being used for farming. It was not surprising that serious surpluses of dairy goods and cereals were accumulating.

Mansholt argued that first of all Western Europe's agricultural labour force should be halved during the 1970s by pensioning off elderly farmers, diverting young and middle-aged farmers to other jobs, and discouraging children from entering the profession unless they were willing to train and become highly qualified.

Secondly, small peasant farms would have to be replaced by large agricultural holdings, growing perhaps 100 ha of cereals or being sufficiently large to support 40–80 dairy cows or 150–200 head of beef cattle. Only 2 per cent of the farms in the Massif Central were of such an order of size.

Thirdly, marketing procedures would need to be modernized and commodity prices readjusted to get rid of surpluses of milk, dairy products, and cereals.

Fourthly, rural land use would have to be drastically reorganized with less being devoted to farming and more to recreation and forestry. Mansholt suggested that the agricultural surface of Western Europe should be cut by 7 per cent by 1980. More recently the Vedel Report on French agriculture has suggested that one-third of French farmland would have to be withdrawn from farming use if the industry was to become efficient in the next two decades. Backward areas in the Common Market would bear the brunt of this reduction whatever its size. The Massif Central falls into such a category, together with Southern Italy, the Alps, the Pyrenees, and other smaller upland areas (Fig. 13). Important changes in the use of rural land must be expected in the future. Upland farming will become increasingly geared to raising beef cattle. Large areas of land will be removed for agricultural use and be devoted to timber and providing recreation facilities for city dwellers. But before looking too far into the future it is necessary to consider the changes that have taken place in the Massif Central in the last two decades.

Fewer farmers, fewer farms

In spite of their backward appearance, agricultural conditions in the Massif Central and other upland areas are changing fast. Many farms are not guaranteed a successor. Thus between 1963 and 1975 the number of holdings in the Massif Central fell from 209 000 to 151 000 (−27 per cent) at a rate exactly equal to the French national average. Most farms are still very small but many have been enlarged as land which falls vacant has been leased or purchased by neighbouring far-

mers. Some 46 per cent of all farms in the Massif Central are over 20 ha and about 12 per cent are over 100 ha (Table 2).

Farm sizes are constantly changing in response to two factors: the high average age of farmers; and the unwillingness of young people to work on the land.

1. The agricultural population is elderly. Many farmers do not have heirs to take over their holdings. Sixty per cent of all the farms in the region in the early 1960s will have disappeared by the early 1980s for this reason. Very poor land has been left to revert to scrub and more will be abandoned in the future. But at the same time young farmers have the chance to purchase or lease more land and enlarge their holdings. The French Government has accelerated this 'natural' process of farm enlargement by offering special pensions to elderly farmers who agree to give up farming and allow their land to be sold or leased to keen young farmers wishing to acquire farms of their own or to neighbours wanting to enlarge their holdings. At first the pensions were only available to farmers aged over 65 but now the age

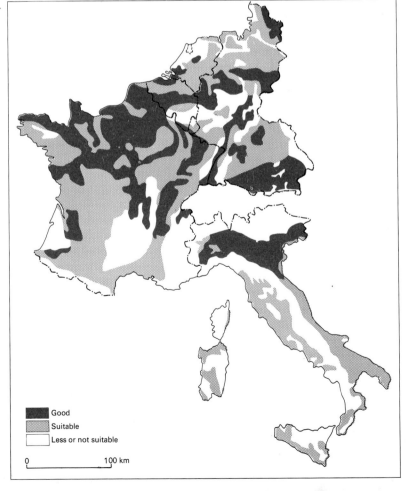

Fig. 13. The quality of land for agriculture in the original six members of the Common Market

Good

Suitable

Less or not suitable

0   100 km

limit has been reduced to 55 years in Brittany, the Alps, the Pyrenees, and the Massif Central. By early 1975 60 000 pensions had been paid out to farmers in the Massif Central, representing about one-sixth of those paid in the whole of France.

2. Young people are moving out of farming since they are not willing to put up with the low standards of living which their parents and grand-parents endured. The Government has intro-duced grants to encourage young people either to abandon farming and take on other jobs or to go to farming college and become properly trained.

Grants for retraining for other jobs are avail-able to farmers and farmworkers under the age of 45. Surprisingly few young people in the Massif have claimed these retraining grants even though large numbers are leaving the land each year. Only 6500 such grants were paid in the region between 1963 and 1975. Four-fifths were to young men under the age of 25 who, after working on their parents' farms, had decided that this was not the life for them. Even the training schemes designed to improve the education of future generations of farmers may have just the reverse

effect and encourage young people to give up farming. Many agricultural colleges are on the margins of towns. Farm children discover a more attractive way of life than they had known at home and many never return to the land.

Co-operatives

Farmers who remain on the land must be en-couraged to join with their neighbours to form co-operatives and pool their knowledge and expertise so that they can run their holdings more efficiently. Co-operatives can be of vital impor-tance for purchasing seeds, fertilizers, and equip-ment, and also for marketing produce at good prices. Many young farmers in the Massif Cen-tral are keen to modernize their farming activities but surprisingly few co-operatives have been set up. Hardly more than four hundred groups of farmers have agreed to organize their work sche-dules in common with their neighbours and pool their skill and machinery to benefit all members of the group. In many instances these arrange-ments simply represent the formalization of exist-ing agreements between family members rather

TABLE 2

Farm size, 1975

| | (percentage of all units) | | | |
	under 5 ha	5–20 ha	20–50 ha	over 50 ha
Massif Central	14	40	34	12
France	30	33	26	11
Nord	25	32	36	7
Picardie	19	18	32	31
Centre	31	19	26	24
Champagne	32	10	21	37
Haute-Normandie	30	29	27	14
Paris Region	30	15	19	36
Basse-Normandie	22	39	30	9
Bretagne	27	44	28	1
Pays de la Loire	27	26	38	9
Poitou-Charentes	29	46	23	2
Auvergne	16	37	32	15
Limousin	11	45	35	9
Aquitaine	28	46	23	3
Midi-Pyrénées	20	40	31	9
Lorraine	38	20	22	20
Alsace	46	35	17	2
Bourgogne	30	21	24	25
Franche-Comté	22	23	40	15
Rhône-Alpes	33	44	18	5
Languedoc	54	32	9	5
Provence/Côte-d'Azur/Corse	62	26	8	4

than being real co-operatives established between completely independent farmers. Aveyron *département* forms something of an exception containing one-quarter of the producer co-operatives in the Massif. One of these has been particularly effective and involves no less than twenty farmers running their holdings in cooperation. Labour, machinery, fertilizers, and other inputs are carefully costed so that each member obtains his appropriate share of the profits at the end of the year.

Co-operatives for marketing, storing, and processing farm products have made considerable progress in the northern parts of the Massif. Half of the farmers in Puy-de-Dôme, Cantal, and Haute-Loire *départements*, who have milk and other dairy products to sell, belong to some kind of co-operative scheme. The best example is the Gerzat co-operative close to Clermont-Ferrand with over 5000 members whose milk is collected and taken to a central dairy for bottling or processing into yoghourt, cream, butter, or powdered milk. Important co-operatives also exist for marketing and slaughtering cattle and for selling meat. They have also been set up in the Limagnes for collecting, storing, and marketing grain. Four-fifths of the cereals grown in Puy-de-Dôme *département* are handled in this way.

Land consolidation

Land consolidation, aimed at grouping small scattered plots of farmland together to create compact units, has taken place in the Limagnes with Government financial assistance since the late 1940s. Almost all of this rich and quite atypical farming area has now been reorganized. Consolidation programmes have been very important in installing new field roads and land drains in this low lying area of open field. Many tiny parcels had fallen out of cultivation because access to them was impossible across neighbours' land. They have now been returned to agricultural use. Apart from the margins of the Limagnes, very little consolidation has been achieved in the higher parts of the Massif Central. Consolidation remains at the project stage in Aveyron and Lozère *départements* but some progress has been achieved elsewhere.

There are three main reasons for this lack of activity. First, the cost of consolidation is high. The State provides the cost of survey work and plot reallocation but it will pay only two-thirds of the remaining costs. These can be extremely high in upland areas where hedges, earth banks, field walls, and trees have to be removed and sunken tracks infilled. The total cost of consolidation per hectare in upland parts of the Massif can be three times that incurred in the Limagnes. Secondly, the future of farming is more certain in the Limagnes than in the impoverished uplands where large areas of land will be devoted to forestry and recreation. Agricultural planners have been far more willing to allocate finance to the lowlands. Thirdly, upland farmers are disillusioned with

A rare example of land consolidation in progress in a middle mountain area about 30 kilometres south-west of Clermont-Ferrand. The hedgerows and earth banks have been removed prior to levelling the ground. Field drains will also be installed

present conditions but many are unwilling to request consolidation which they still greet with either overt or concealed hostility. The ideal reaction following land consolidation is to provoke a feeling of 'hunger' for more land amongst farmers as they begin to appreciate the potentialities offered by mechanized farming and seek to enlarge their holdings to make mechanization more effective. Unfortunately this reaction is rare. In most cases upland farmers are glad to use their new field roads but are slow to improve their farming practices.

Farm enlargement: the SAFERs

The task of planning farm enlargement has been entrusted to the SAFER* organizations set up in the 1960s. Eight SAFERs are responsible for the various parts of the Massif Central. These organizations have the somewhat contradictory aims of enlarging existing farms, creating new 'viable' units (which are sufficiently large to employ two people full-time throughout the year), avoiding speculation in land prices, and safeguarding the family character of French farming. The SAFERs have powers to purchase farmland as it comes freely on to the market and then to control its resale to guarantee farm enlargement or the creation of new holdings for young men wanting farms of their own. In addition, the SAFERs acquire some of the land surrendered by elderly farmers when they receive I.V.D. pensions. The land is passed into a 'land bank' and may be kept there for up to five years when improvements are carried out such as draining, hedgerow removal, road installation, and the construction of buildings. All sales of farmland require the approval of the local SAFER. This may be withheld if proposals do not fit with the SAFER's conception of what use could best be made of the land in question.

Demand for land is slight in many upland parts of the Massif Central as a result of decades of depopulation. In any case farmland is lower in quality than in most other parts of France. As a result, property is cheap and SAFERs in the Massif Central can operate at relatively little expense. Costs involved in the acquisition and resale of each hectare of land are only one-third of those recorded in Alsace, Lower Normandy, and parts of the Paris Basin and SAFERs operating in the Auvergne and the Aveyron have been amongst the most active in France. Nevertheless inadequate finance imposes a more serious restriction on their work than local hostility or apathy. The SAFERs have had greatest success in creating farms between 20 ha and 50 ha in

*Société d'Aménagement Foncier et d'Etablissement Rural.

size. The latter are still small properties when measured against the standards set by Dr. Mansholt. Forty per cent of the farms enlarged or created by the SAFERs were returned to farmers under 35 years of age. This represents a very important move for bringing down the average age of farmers in the Massif Central since only 5 per cent were in that age group in 1967.

The SAFERs have expressed doubts about the effectiveness of their operations since they interfere with the normal process of competition for land between small and large farms. Under free market conditions owners of large farms are usually in a far stronger position for increasing the size of their holdings than are their smaller neighbours. The SAFERs are in fact slowing down the normal evolution of large farms into very large ones, since their aim is always to establish 'viable' family farms that will support two men full-time throughout the year. These may be suitable family farms for the present but they will be much too small to be really viable in the future. SAFERs in the Massif Central are wondering whether they are simply creating problem farms for the 1980s.

Integrated rural planning: the SOMIVAL

In 1962 the SOMIVAL* planning corporation was founded at Clermont-Ferrand to undertake research and to propose and implement integrated schemes for rural management in association with other official and private organizations in the Massif Central. The SOMIVAL originally operated in the Auvergne region and Corrèze *département*. In recent years Creuse and Haute-Vienne *départements* have also benefited from its activities. The real importance of the SOMIVAL, as of other rural planning corporations in France, and of bodies such as the Highlands and Islands Development Board in Scotland, stems from their ability to tackle the problems of the countryside in an integrated fashion which overcomes the limitations of individual Government departments with restricted fields of responsibility. The SOMIVAL operates to tackle the interlinked problems of improving farming, rationalizing afforestation, and developing tourism. Each of these themes will be considered in turn.

Agricultural improvement

The SOMIVAL runs pilot farms and is concerned with modernizing crop production and animal rearing. Experimental irrigation schemes in the Limagnes have shown that yields of maize, fodder crops, tobacco, and soft fruit can be raised signi-

*Société pour la Mise en Valeur de l'Auvergne-Limousin.

ficantly through rational watering. Over 100 000 ha of farmland in the valleys of the Allier, Cher, and Loire would benefit from irrigation. The SOMIVAL has also undertaken experimental livestock breeding in the mountain zone to replace traditional breeds of sheep and cattle with others which yield high quality meat. Excellent Charolais beef cattle are also being bred in Allier *département*.

Management plans have been prepared for individual villages and for complete agricultural regions so that rural land may be zoned for rational use in the future. A serious problem is posed by large areas of communal land, owned collectively by hamlets and villages in the mountains and used in the past for grazing flocks of sheep and goats and herds of cattle. These high areas are now seriously under-used and only one-third of the communal pastures of the Massif are still grazed. An equal amount is tree-covered and the remainder is uncultivated moorland and scrub. The SOMIVAL is helping highland communities to draw up plans to put their communal land into use for seasonal grazing or afforestation.

The corporation works in close association with the SAFER and other rural organizations to implement its rural management plans. A good example of such co-operation is provided by the management of high summer pastures in the volcanic uplands of the Cantal and Puy-de-Dôme *départements*. In the past these areas above the limit of permanent settlement were used by individual farmers from lowland and middle-mountain areas for grazing transhumant cattle in summer and producing cheese. This type of land use declined in importance after World War II since it was very difficult for farmers to find sufficient stockmen to look after each small herd during the summer. Farmworkers were no longer willing to endure the loneliness and poor conditions involved in living in the *burons*. As a result, transhumant grazing became very rare in the 1950s. A small group of young farmers in the Cantal were determined to modernize the system by establishing ranches where small herds from individual farms could be organized into a large co-operative herd and managed by a small number of expert stockmen.

In 1960 many high pastures in the Cantal had been abandoned entirely. Grassland quality had deteriorated as rough scrubby vegetation invaded areas which previously had been grazed on a regular annual basis. Fences, walls, and *burons* were in a bad state of repair. Fragmented ownership of the *montagnes* added to the problems which would have to be solved if ranches were to

be set up. The local SAFER has played an important role by purchasing land and creating large 200 ha blocks which have been fenced into 30–40 ha units for grazing in rotation. With the help of the SOMIVAL new access roads have been built, *burons* reconstructed, pastures reseeded, and water piped to them. Wind-breaks have been planted where site conditions are not too harsh.

Two ranches have been set up in the Cantal. At first only 150 cattle were moved up to the *montagnes* in a co-operative herd. Now the venture has become much more popular and more than 1200 cattle are being grazed on ranches each year. Vaccination is compulsory for livestock entering co-operative herds and veterinary advice is readily available. Cattle are sent from farms in lower parts of the Cantal around Aurillac where farmers are taking advantage of the resources of the high mountains to supplement fodder supplies from their own farms. Home-produced fodder can now be kept for feeding to the stock in winter. Co-operative schemes of this kind have started in other parts of the Massif Central and involve sheep as well as cattle. They provide good examples of old systems of agricultural activity, in this instance transhumance, being modernized to meet present-day requirements.

Forestry

Afforestation provides an important solution to the problem of under-used upland areas throughout Europe. Physical conditions in all but the very highest areas of the Massif Central are ideal for growing trees. Since 1900 the woodland cover has doubled and now occupies one-fifth of the land area of the Massif. Large areas of *landes* still remain in spite of this, and uncultivated areas are being added every year as the farming population declines and land falls out of agricultural use. Afforestation might be envisaged over much of this unproductive land.

Most of the afforestation which has taken place in the Massif Central since the beginning of the century has been very disorganized. The French forestry authorities may not plan or undertake the planting of trees on blocks of land smaller than 25 ha. But private landowners, who own 80 per cent of the present woodland in the Massif, are free to plant up even the tiniest piece of land. Many absentee landowners, who have inherited land but are unable to use it themselves or are unwilling to lease it to neighbouring farmers, have done just this. 'Postage-stamp' afforestation has occurred in many parts of the Massif. Land use chaos has resulted. Farmers who try to grow crops or maintain good pastures round the afforested plots find that their land is invaded by pests and weeds. Shadow-effects hamper plant growth and natural drainage is disturbed. Schemes for land consolidation and farm enlargement are hindered and made extremely expensive where 'postage-stamp' woodland has to be cleared away.

Another problem is linked to the fact that much of the woodland in the Massif Central does not produce the kinds of timber which are currently in demand. More than half of the woodland cover is deciduous and yields hardwoods which were needed for domestic firewood and carpentry in the traditional economy. Demands for such timber scarcely exist any more because of de-population and changing methods of heating and building. Softwoods are needed instead for pro-ducing paper and cellulose. Forestry planners have the difficult task of trying to encourage landowners to replace their deciduous woodland with conifers.

Various forms of action have been taken to try to remedy these problems. The SOMIVAL has co-operated with other forestry planners to ana-lyse physical, demographic, and economic condi-tions in order to find out which parts of the Massif Central are best suited for growing timber. Parti-cular attention is paid to soils and climatic condi-tions, farms which are likely to have no successors to operate them, and any weaknesses in local rural economies. As a result of these investigations areas of land are zoned according to their aptitude for farming or tree-growing in the future. Such zon-ing schemes are of value in helping planners to decide whether to encourage programmes of agricultural improvement (such as land consoli-dation or farm enlargement) or to concentrate on obtaining finance necessary for afforestation. Un-fortunately it is not possible to ensure that land-owners actually use their property to conform with zoning proposals. The success of land use zoning depends on goodwill and the influence of planners in convincing landowners of the need to rationalize upland management.

Afforestation schemes are supported by three types of financial help: direct grants, loans, and long-term contracts with landowners wishing to plant trees. Grants are the cheapest form of financial aid to administer since expensive pre-liminary planning is not required. Unfortunately the end products are the least satisfactory. In the last decade the average size of afforestation project in the Massif Central financed by grants was only 1·5 ha. More often than not such tiny areas were 'postage stamp' woodlands contributing to fur-ther land use chaos. Only rarely did they fill in 'holes' in existing areas of woodland. Loans and

French Government Tourist Office
Small, irregularly shaped patches of land have been afforested in many upland parts of the Massif Central, including this area of the Corrèze. A complicated mixture of woodland, scrub, permanent pasture, and arable land makes agricultural restructuring not only difficult but extremely costly

long-term contracts give far more satisfactory results since preliminary planning is required before they are awarded. Only large blocks of land are authorized for afforestation and these are in areas which have been zoned for timber produc-tion.

Another major problem facing forestry plan-ners is the need to consolidate tiny plots of land into larger blocks before tree-planting takes place. The most desirable way to do this is by setting up *groupements forestiers*. Individuals sacrifice direct ownership claims to their personal plots of land when they join a *groupement* but their heirs will enjoy a proportion of the profits when the timber reaches maturity after having borne their fair share of the expenses. Such *groupements* are un-fortunately still in their infancy in the Massif Central. Their establishment is slowed down by the unwillingness of landowners to join together in this way and also by a host of legal complica-tions which restrict the work of the SOMIVAL and other rural planners.

Most of the technical problems involved in tree-planting in the Massif Central have been overcome after careful research into the tolerance limits of softwood species. The problems that remain involve the unwillingness of small land-owners to join with their neighbours to undertake rational afforestation. One major hindrance stems from the fact that the profits from afforestation are not enjoyed until the trees reach maturity, are felled, and sold, 40 or 50 years after they have been planted. The SOMIVAL recommends that two lines of action be taken to encourage a faster rate of afforestation. Lump sums might be paid which would more than cover the landowners' planting expenses, or else 'salaries' could be paid from guaranteed buyers who would have signed contracts to acquire the timber when it reaches maturity. It is clear that some kind of arrangement will have to be drawn up to accelerate afforestation in upland areas throughout Western Europe if Dr. Mansholt's proposals for withdrawing land from agricultural use are to be implemented.

Recreation

The Massif Central and other upland areas will always be at an agricultural disadvantage compared with lowland parts of Europe but, as relatively undeveloped regions, they offer certain attractions for recreation. The Massif Central contains an important heritage of Romanesque architecture, thermal springs, small snowfields for winter sports, and lakes and rivers for fishing, sailing, and swimming. Its main attraction is as an oasis of relative peace and quiet which contrasts with the noise and overcrowding of modern city life. The region is within easy access of Paris and several other major French cities but it is avoided by most foreign tourists as they speed southwards along main routes to the Mediterranean sun. Some parts of the Massif, such as the Morvan, are already important recreation areas for Parisians. Undoubtedly the region can draw great benefit from its recreational resources but there are very real climatic limitations to the attractiveness of this upland area for holidaymaking. The Massif Central is not in the same class as the major tourist areas of Western Europe and cannot hope to compete with the sunshine of the Mediterranean, the snowfields of the Alps, or the cheapness of Spain.

The region contains 400 of the 1200 mineral springs in France and attracts one-third of all the *curistes* who take the waters in France (Fig. 14). But this branch of tourism has decreased in popularity since 1945 and offers little prospect of future growth. Hotels in the spa towns no longer receive the large and prosperous clientele that they accommodated in the past. Each spa town is now concerned with diversifying its economic base and introducing new forms of employment. Vichy has undoubtedly made the greatest progress in this respect and will be considered in detail later.

By contrast with the decline of thermalism, other types of recreation and tourism are becoming increasingly popular in the Massif Central. Winter sports form an important growth industry with the number of skiers in France currently rising by 10 per cent each year. The Massif does not contain snowfields comparable with those in the Alps but a number of ski centres have developed successfully. The Col du Lioran in the Cantal was established as a winter sports centre as early as 1911. This example was quite exceptional and owed its early development to the fact that its railway station opened directly on to the snowfields and was served by trains from Paris.

The real growth of snow resorts in the Massif Central dates only from the 1960s. In 1961 Super-Lioran was modernized and additional accommodation provided for skiers. Special trains leave Paris on Friday nights in winter which allow Parisians to enjoy a weekend's skiing in the Cantal and to return to the capital in time for work on Monday. Super-Besse is another example of a success story. In 1960 only a single *buron* stood on the site which it now occupies. Since then ski lifts have been installed and hotels, chalets, and holiday villages built to provide accommodation for 3000 winter sports enthusiasts. The nearby spa town of Mont-Dore has diversified its activities by improving access to local snowfields and by providing accommodation for a winter sports clientele. Other ski centres have been developed on a less spectacular scale in the Forez and Mezenc highlands to cater for the growing popularity of skiing among town-dwellers in the Massif.

The tourism division of the SOMIVAL has been important in helping local communities make the best use of their attractions for recreation. Over thirty holiday villages in which chalets are available for letting were built by the corporation between 1966 and 1975. Together they can accommodate 8000 holiday makers at any one time. More villages are being built with the help of the SOMIVAL. Unfortunately the holiday season is relatively short in areas away from the snowfields. Various schemes for accommodating workers and students in the chalets during the off-season have not met with success. A second type of development by the SOMIVAL involves building estates of second homes for purchase by individual families. Ten estates have already been completed and can accommodate 3400 people. More developments of this kind are in progress.

Sometimes the holiday villages and estates of second homes are just parts of larger recreation schemes with camping grounds, tennis courts, swimming pools, and boating lakes. Reservoirs retained by hydro-electric power barrages on major rivers such as the Dordogne provide good sites for recreation centres. Successful schemes are in operation at Bort-les-Orgues (Dordogne) and Saint-Etienne-Cantalès (Cère) but only after long and costly legal wrangling with landowners on the lakeshores. In addition to making use of existing water surfaces, the SOMIVAL has flooded eight valleys to create lakes for swimming and water sports. Five more are under construction.

Other forms of recreation attraction are being developed. The fourth French national park was created in the Cévennes in Autumn 1970. The inner zone of 84 000 ha has only 650 inhabitants and will be preserved as far as possible from any kind of change. Limited development, including accommodation, will be permitted in the surrounding 200 000 ha of the national park. Other areas have been set aside as regional parks in the volcanic uplands west of Clermont-Ferrand, the Morvan, Mont Pilat close to Saint-Etienne, and Haut-Languedoc. A similar park has been pro-

posed for the depopulated Montagne Limousine in the late 1970s. By creating these parks planners hope to prevent the degradation of visually attractive landscapes through haphazard private development and yet be able to provide well-designed facilities for recreation. Regional parks have been welcomed enthusiastically by town dwellers in the Massif but have aroused opposition from country landowners, who fear that their property will be invaded by weekenders and holidaymakers.

In addition to these planned forms of recreation facility, many second homes have been established in the Massif Central for weekend and holiday occupation by city dwellers. More than one-third of all dwellings are used as second homes in some areas around Clermont-Ferrand and Saint-Etienne. Similarly the Morvan is now well-established as a weekend recreation area for Parisians. But second homes are found in other areas apart from those close to large cities and possess-

Fig. 14. Aspects of tourism in the Massif Central

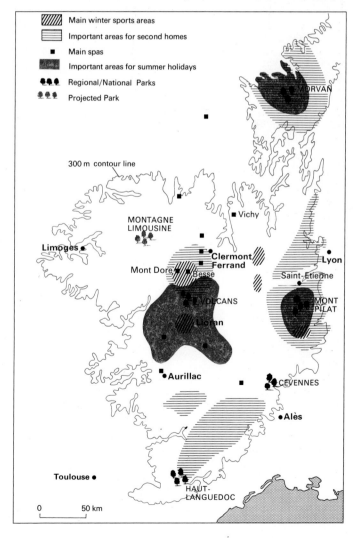

ing attractive landscapes. Many migrants who left the Massif when they were young are still sentimentally attached to their home villages, where they either inherit or purchase houses for leisure-time use and perhaps eventually for retirement.

Some rural communities are strongly in favour of diversifying their economic activities by catering for weekenders and tourists. Such villages and small towns have made great efforts to increase accommodation, provide tracks for skiers to reach distant snowfields, or create artificial lakes for water sports in this land-locked region. By contrast, other communities are opposed to the presence of weekenders and holidaymakers and have made no attempts to cater for their needs. Nevertheless important efforts are being made in many parts of the Massif Central to develop the 'recreation business' into an important economic activity. Over the last five years the region's accommodation capacity has been increased by one-quarter in hotels, holiday villages, and camping grounds.

Changing settlement patterns

More than half of the inhabitants of the Massif Central still live in rural areas with declining population totals. Rates of loss have been most severe from small villages, hamlets, and isolated farms whilst larger villages and small towns have declined less rapidly and in some cases have managed to retain their population. Land resources will continue to require farmers and foresters to manage them in the future but this will involve far fewer people than at present. Adequate services will have to be provided for these country dwellers but will not be available at every village. Shops, schools, and other services have already disappeared from many small settlements in the Massif Central which are linked by long stretches of little-used roads that require costly maintenance in a harsh climatic environment.

Regional planners have attempted to rationalize the present process of service contraction by selecting certain small towns as 'holding points' where basic services such as medium quality shops, a secondary school, a local agricultural college, a bank, a doctor, an old people's home, a sports field, and a community hall will be guaranteed. This type of policy is being implemented in many rural areas elsewhere in Europe. Patterns of central places and their hinterlands have been investigated in the Massif Central to select settlements where financial assistance should be concentrated for building up services to the required

level. A process of 'natural selection' has operated and some small towns have emerged almost 'automatically' as local service centres. But this is not always the case and planners have the difficult task of choosing between villages and small towns to decide which should be equipped for stability or even growth in the future and which should be condemned to decline.

Planners have tried to define a network of settlements with a sufficient number of 'holding points' so that residents in every part of the Massif Central will be able to reach their local service centre within 30 minutes' driving time. An orderly, regular pattern of holding points does not emerge because of local differences in the existing pattern and density of settlement, the poor quality of many country roads in difficult terrain, and the very real hazards involved in driving in the mountains in bad weather. However, hinterlands with diameters of 40–60 kms have been defined which contain between 10 000 and 20 000 residents apiece. The equipment of 'holding points' with a range of basic services will not only benefit permanent residents but should also provide suitable centres for developing tourism and installing light industry in an attempt to diversify rural economies.

Regional differences in rural improvement

Rural improvements have not been spread evenly throughout the Massif Central. Sharp contrasts exist between neighbouring villages and adjacent agricultural areas. Important innovations in farming or tourism may have occurred at one place but surrounding settlements only a few kilometres away appear impervious to change. In spite of this, four rural sub-regions can be recognized in the Massif Central.

The western uplands

The western uplands from Limousin to the Causses are severely depopulated. Farming in Limousin is directed even more strongly to cattle-rearing for beef and veal. Large areas of uncultivated land are being afforested. The traditional sheep-rearing economy in the Causses for the manufacture of ewes' milk cheese at Roquefort is also under-going change. Local supplies of labour are declining in many places and are no longer sufficient to milk the ewes. Some farms in the Causses no longer rear sheep for their milk but only for their meat and wool. Others have been enlarged and modernized and still dispatch ewes' milk to the cheese makers of Roquefort. A few very large farms have been set up which are fully modernized and milk their ewes by machine.

Seriously depopulated parts of the Causses have been abandoned to tree-growing or grazing transhumant sheep, which are brought into the mountains from Languedoc each summer.

The volcanic mountain zone

Cattle-rearing is increasingly the main concentration in the volcanic mountain zone. Few crops of any kind are grown, apart from potatoes for family consumption. Traditional breeds of cattle such as the hardy Aubrac and Salers remain popular but new breeds have also been introduced. High summer pastures are used less intensively than in the past but co-operative ranches operate on some *montagnes*. Other upland pastures are used for fattening Charolais and Limousin beef cattle and for grazing transhumant sheep from Languedoc. Important winter sports facilities have been installed and summer holidaymakers are attracted to the volcanic lakes and the 'lunar landscape' of the Chaîne des Puys.

The plateaux and middle-mountain areas

Very important local contrasts are shown in the plateaux and middle-mountain areas. Agricultural innovations are rare in Livradois and the Cévennes where depopulation has been severe and the remaining elderly population rejects change. But progress has been made in other areas. Important improvements have taken place in the Morvan as a result of land consolidation, mechanization of arable farming, and careful breeding of high-quality livestock. In addition, the area is close enough to Paris to attract many weekenders who introduce social and economic changes as they occupy their second homes. The Monts du Lyonnais have established important contacts with nearby industrial towns, which act as markets for local farm products and also provide sources of capital and initiative for modernizing rural life.

Perhaps the greatest progress has been made in the Ségala district around the market town of Rodez (25 000 inhabitants). Traditionally this was an impoverished rye-growing area, contrasting with the wheat-producing plains of Aquitaine. Railway construction in the early twentieth century allowed lime to be brought in to improve the acid soils. Wheat replaced rye as the staple crop. Since 1945 important innovations have stemmed from Rodez with its agricultural co-operatives,

The rural economy of the Roquefort area of the Causses, based on the manufacture of ewes' milk cheese, is one of the most distinctive in the whole of the Massif Central

advisory services, and a centre for the artificial insemination of livestock. Local breeds of beef and dairy cattle have been greatly improved, and hybrid maize and ley grass provide high quality fodder. Unlike most parts of the Massif Central, the Ségala has a rational mechanized farming system and uses large quantities of fertilizer.

The lowland troughs

The lowland troughs of the Limagnes and Forez are exceptions to the general rule of rural backwardness in the Massif Central. Features of agricultural progress, such as co-operatives and land consolidation, are particularly well developed. These areas are also experiencing important population growth and urbanization. Farming in the Limagnes is turning increasingly from cereal-growing to livestock-rearing, with Charolais beef cattle in the north and dairy cattle within the Clermont-Ferrand milkshed. Large sections of agricultural land in both lowland areas will have to be sacrificed in the future to accommodate housing and industrial estates around Clermont-Ferrand and Saint-Etienne.

4 Planning the Massif Central: Industrial and Urban Areas

Industrial planning

European governments have introduced many forms of financial help to assist old industrial areas attract new factories and to try to disperse industrial dynamism from economically healthy regions to less developed ones. In 1955 special grants were made available to help install new factories in a dozen industrial 'black spots' throughout France, which included Limoges, Montceau-les-Mines, and Thiers in the Massif Central. Local authorities in the region offered tax reductions and other incentives to industrialists. At the same time factory owners and craftsmen in these 'crisis areas' attempted to diversify and modernize their production.

The cutlers of Thiers took two types of action: advertising the high quality of their craftsman-made goods, but also diversifying the range of products made in the town. New factories have been opened and old workshops converted to producing plastics, household equipment, fittings for cars and planes, keys, as well as mass-produced stainless steel cutlery. Efforts have been made to simplify the organization of work in the cutlery trade and a dozen master cutlers have standardized techniques of production and marketing. Their efforts have paid off and half of their output is exported. In recent years the town has entered a new phase of prosperity, but it is still proud of its claim to produce 21 000 different types of cutting edge. Other industrial problem areas have been less successful than Thiers. Certainly very little industrial diversification was achieved at Limoges until the 1960s.

Grants were also available for establishing factories in other parts of the Massif. Until 1964 these were awarded according to the merits of individual schemes and the severity of employment problems in specific localities. Development grants and tax relief for new factories were then reorganized on a geographical basis with the highest rates being available in a small number of towns, including Limoges. Highland parts of the Massif Central were guaranteed financial help for factory installation. Old industrial areas such as Alès, Montluçon, and Saint-Etienne benefited from 'adaptation grants' to help revitalize their local economy. The lowland trough of the Allier valley already had a buoyant economy and was excluded from financial assistance for factory installation. In 1967 more advantageous grants and loans were introduced to encourage the creation of factory jobs throughout the Massif Central which was recognized as a Rural Renovation Zone. Industrial reconversion bureaux were opened in the same year to help bring new jobs to Alès and Saint-Etienne.

The end result of all these schemes has been disappointing. Government finance is not available for industrial development in the greater part of the Limagnes but that is where most new factories have been opened, producing car parts, electrical goods, domestic equipment, and clothing. *Route Nationale* 9 provides easy communication between Paris and Clermont-Ferrand and is rapidly becoming an important industrial artery lined with new factories. Allier *département*, centred on Moulins only 270 km from the capital, has experienced by far the most vigorous industrial growth in recent years with 26 new factories opened between 1962 and 1965 creating 3000 new jobs. The city of Limoges also underwent important industrial development in the 1960s as a result of direct State action in opening a nationalized car works.

Little has been achieved in the high parts of the Massif Central even though virtually every small town has attempted to set up its own industrial estate in the hope of attracting factory owners. Some schemes have succeeded and light industries have been installed. The best example is the area between Le Puy and Saint-Etienne where many new factories producing clothing, electrical goods, and domestic equipment have opened in recent years. Unfortunately many 'industrial estates' in the Massif Central are still without factories. Some of those which have opened have encountered problems of recruiting a suitable labour force in the immediate vicinity. Housing may not be available for managers and key personnel used to better living standards in urban areas. Rather than hoping that such a scatter of industrial estates could ever be a success it would be more realistic to plan a limited number of industrial zones at selected 'holding points' which would be the centres of broad commuting zones drawing on labour from the countryside and from surrounding small towns as well.

Recent attempts to industrialize rural parts of the Massif Central have met with limited success. Significant industrial growth has taken place only in such areas as the Allier trough and Limoges which are marginal to the mountain mass and are on good road and rail links to Paris. Population and economic activities still drain away from the high Massif as they did in the past.

Adaptation grants are available to encourage the creation of new factories in old industrial areas and special industrial reconversion bureaux exist at Alès and Saint-Etienne to undertake research, to propose, and then to implement measures to help solve local employment problems. Information on existing labour trends has to be co-ordinated to measure actual and latent unemployment. The facilities of the industrial areas (such as labour supply, empty factories, and new industrial estates) need to be publicized together with the complicated forms of financial assistance available to incoming industrialists. Much depends on the initiative of key members of the bureaux in gaining the confidence of local workers, employers, and administrators, and of industrialists who may be encouraged to move in from other regions. To obtain this degree of liaison the bureaux work in close consultation with central planners in Paris.

The bureaux have been instrumental in negotiating new jobs in both industrial areas. New factories have been built on industrial estates at Alès and Saint-Etienne and a proportion of the jobs has been reserved for ex-miners and workers released from local industries such as textiles and metallurgy. Two major problems remain. First, it has been easier to attract light industries requiring female employees than firms needing male workers. Even if suitable replacement jobs can be found, many ex-miners and workers from heavy industries are having to go through a difficult re-adjustment period not simply involving a change-over to work in light industry or in a service activity but also finding a new focus for their social life which had previously been centred on the factory or the mine.

Secondly, the bureaux have had limited success in persuading firms from Paris and other dynamic parts of France to open factories in the Massif. Taking the example of Saint-Etienne, three-quarters of the firms established by the bureaux in new factories have come from the city itself and represent a process of decongestion and expansion away from cramped industrial quarters in Saint-Etienne. The old industrial areas of the Massif are unfortunately not proving as attractive to outside firms as had previously been hoped.

Urban planning

Only 45 per cent of the population of the region lived in towns in 1968, by contrast with 70 per cent for the whole of France. Only Saint-Etienne, Clermont-Ferrand, and Limoges have more than 100 000 inhabitants. Each is marginal to the mountain core of the Massif. This is particularly true of the Saint-Etienne urban area with a total population of 500 000. At an altitude of 500 metres it lies within the physical boundary of the Massif Central. But in spite of its large size it has not developed an important service hinterland. This is due to four main reasons. First, the city is only 40 km from the river Rhône and as such is right on the eastern margin of the mountain mass. Secondly, it is situated on the watershed between the Rhône and the Loire drainage basins so that routeways diverge from it rather than converge towards it (in contrast with Lyon to the east). Thirdly, its growth has been due to coal-mining and manufacturing not to service provision. Finally, it is overshadowed as a service centre by the 'millionaire' city of Lyon only 50 km away.

Clermont-Ferrand with 250 000 inhabitants is in many respects the opposite of Saint-Etienne. It is located on the major routeway from Paris into the mountain zone at a point where east/west routes across the Massif converge upon north/south ones. In such a position it functions as a centre for the north-central part of the Massif containing a wide variety of retail and wholesale facilities. Until recently it was the only university city in the Massif. Limoges serves a much smaller hinterland further to the west.

The southern half of the Massif has no major regional centre within its borders and looks to Toulouse and Montpellier for specialized services such as university education. Local administrative towns (*préfectures*), such as Le Puy, Aurillac, and Rodez (Fig. 4) with 20 000–30 000 inhabitants, provide most services. By virtue of their isolation in mountainous country and their distance from large cities these medium-sized towns support a surprising range of administrative, educational, retail, and manufacturing functions. They are important market centres at the hub of bus networks which serve wide areas. The existence of these *préfecture* towns accounts for the relatively high proportion of workers in tertiary activities in their respective *départements*.

Every town in the Massif is attempting to diversify its economic activities. Market centres and *préfecture* towns are trying to attract modern industries and increase their range of service functions. These aims are also shared by Limoges and Saint-Etienne as they try to compensate for

Vichy

the contraction of their staple industries. Both have benefited in recent years from State action in creating new universities. These two cities, together with Clermont-Ferrand, are large enough to experience town-planning problems involving the renewal of inner areas and the management of suburban estates. Vichy exemplifies another type of town in search of new activities to compensate for the decline of its spa.

Vichy

The traditional spa trade lasted for five months each year, when the town's population doubled. Unfortunately the fashion for taking the waters has declined in importance since World War II and especially since decolonization in the 1950s and early 1960s. Large numbers of Frenchmen no longer come from North Africa to Vichy each year for the benefit of their health. Some of the town's luxurious hotels have been divided into flats; and expensive shops that stayed open all year on the profits of a few months' trade have closed their doors.

In recent years Vichy has formed a development corporation to introduce new activities to the town. Its plan is threefold: to install sports and recreation facilities for use throughout the year that might attract young and healthy people to the town as well as the elderly and the sick, and thereby counterbalance future contraction of the spa trade; to introduce manufacturing; and to provide the town with an educational function in the winter months.

The first aim is being realized at a specially built sports complex alongside the river Allier which has been dammed by a new barrage to create a 120 ha lake for championship rowing, sailing, and water skiing. Other recreational facilities in the Omnisports Park include swimming pools, football pitches, and a race track. To achieve the second aim an industrial estate has been set up with factories producing light metal goods, food products, clothing, and medicinal preparations in addition to bottling Vichy-Etat mineral water. An international language school was opened in 1964 and provides the town with an important educational role. Other training centres have been added in recent years.

In addition to these achievements of Vichy town council, the Perrier corporation—which manages the spa, casino, parks, and many entertainment facilities under contract to the State, and thus makes Vichy something of a 'company town' —is modernizing the spa to attract *curistes* in the final quarter of the twentieth century. The enchanting setting of Vichy remains, but the fashionable nobility, the colonials, and glittering Eastern princes have departed, their places being taken by smaller, plainer crowds of *sécurité sociale* patients.

Limoges

The city of Limoges with a population of 150 000 has been an industrial problem area for the greater part of the present century, following the contraction of the porcelain industry the workforce of which declined from 10 000 in 1901 to 2500 in 1961. Even this small number was only maintained by the introduction of porcelain-using industries such as the manufacture of electrical switching gear. Limoges did not form an attractive focus for rural migrants and its population scarcely increased in the first half of the twentieth century. The city council did little to improve housing, parks, roads, water supplies, or mains drainage prior to 1960. The left-wing politics of Limoges were frowned upon by the Paris Government and finances for urban improvement were not made available. The city lacked a university and young people had to go elsewhere in France to pursue their studies. They rarely returned to Limoges when they qualified because suitable jobs were lacking in this depressed industrial city. Even with the allocation of special grants for industrial development very few new jobs were created in the 1950s.

By contrast, the 1960s witnessed important

changes in the city. Three major improvements in employment have taken place. In 1964 the old arsenal which employed 1200 persons was transferred to the nationalized S.A.V.I.E.M.-Renault vehicle corporation. Now 3000 workers are employed in this dynamic industry. They receive higher wages than employees in the city's other factories. In the early 1960s the postal authorities installed new offices and educational services in the city. A national centre for handling post-office financial transactions was set up, together with a large training centre for post-office workers. More than 1000 new jobs were created. A four-faculty university and a regional teaching hospital were established and hundreds of new jobs made available for local people. Teaching and research posts have been filled by trained personnel from other parts of France but secretarial and domestic staff have been recruited locally and buildings have been constructed by local contractors. Each of these major improvements was achieved as a result of direct intervention by the State after decades of neglect.

During the 1960s the city administration made great progress in improving living conditions in Limoges. New highways were built and a start made on renovating the oldest parts of the city. A ring of industrial estates has been set up on the city margins, together with large new housing estates. More than 10 000 flats and houses were built around the city in a decade. Such dynamism was quite unknown in the previous half century.

Saint-Etienne

The Saint-Etienne urban area, with 500 000 inhabitants, contains the largest city in the Massif Central and provides a classic example of a *maladjusted* area (Fig. 15). Its growth stemmed from coal-mining and metallurgy. But coal output fell from over 4 million tons in 1940 to less than 1·5 million tons in 1972, and mining continued to be run down. Already the labour force in the coal industry had been cut from 21 500 in 1945 to less than 7000 in 1969. The coalfield had been mechanized and modernized since World War II, with one massive thermal power station serving the region in place of five, and one vast cokeworks instead of three. The Givors power station was opened on the banks of the Rhône in 1965 to consume unsaleable supplies of coal from Saint-Etienne. In spite of such efforts the coal industry has lost the energy battle: against natural gas from Lacq which has been piped to the city since 1959, and against petroleum whose role was strengthened when the Feyzin refinery was opened near Lyon in 1964.

French Government Tourist Office

Porcelain manufacture in Limoges

Three planning objectives have been established for Saint-Etienne: to revitalize existing economic activities, to introduce new ones, and to renovate the city's built-environment. The task of reviving coal-mining has proved impossible and there are serious doubts regarding the prospects of other industries such as textiles and metallurgy. Immediately after World War II proposals for rationalizing the company structure and productive capacity of the French iron and steel industry were announced in the Monnet Plan. Reactions were slow at Saint-Etienne and not until 1953 were mergers completed to produce the C.A.F.L.* which now dominates the local metallurgical industry. The Saint-Etienne region thus did not benefit from the first wave of post-war industrial modernization unlike the metallurgical region around Le Creusot to the north. Le Creusot is a 'company town' dominated by the Schneider corporation which, from the late nineteenth century, worked progressively away from ordinary steel-making and metallurgy to specialize in the production of high-quality goods such as stainless steels, steels for locomotives and other machines, and arms. Saint-Etienne was still widening the range of goods it produced at this time. At present the C.A.F.L. is transferring some of its production of quality steels to the modernized S.F.A.C.† (part of the Schneider

*Compagnie des Ateliers et Forges de la Loire.
†Société des Forges et Ateliers du Creusot.

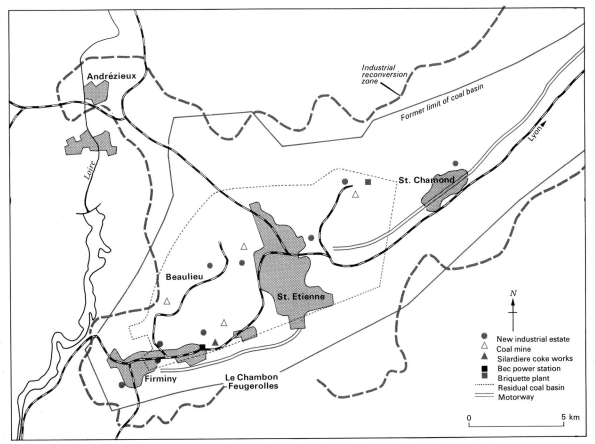

Fig. 15. The Saint-Etienne industrial basin

group) which has reduced its labour force during the 1960s. By contrast, numbers of metallurgical workers increased over the same period at Saint-Etienne, but this trend may not continue since the region is handicapped by a much less thorough rationalization than that which has taken place at Le Creusot and is now paying dearly for the time lost in the modernization phase of the late 1940s and 1950s.

All branches of the textile trade at Saint-Etienne have been shedding labour with the workforce falling from 45 000 in 1938 to under 25 000 in 1969. Between one-third and one-half of the present number will be lost by the early 1980s. The city's industrial reconversion bureau has experienced less success in creating new jobs than had previously been anticipated. But the recent opening of a university has served to diversify Saint-Etienne's economic activities and create much-needed non-industrial employment.

Urban renovation is essential since Saint-Etienne still contains a high proportion of poor housing constructed during the nineteenth century industrialization phase. Work has been

started on reconstructing inner areas of Saint-Etienne and neighbouring industrial communities. A new educational, cultural, and shopping centre (known as Saint-Etienne II) is being constructed south of the old city centre. New housing estates have been built at Beaulieu and Firminy-Vert on the surrounding plateaux above the smoke and grime of the industrial basin.

Two new problems have developed in the Saint-Etienne conurbation. A motorway has been built between the city and Lyon 50 km to the north-east and inter-city rail services have been improved. These developments have created an imbalance in Saint-Etienne. Industrial firms from Lyon which have opened new factories at Saint-Etienne have constructed them close to the motorway to the east of the city centre. Unfortunately the problem of contracting job opportunities is most serious in the western part of the conurbation and it would be most desirable for replacement jobs to be installed there.

A second problem stems from the configuration of the industrial basin. Few sites for new factories are available close to the built-up area of Saint-

42

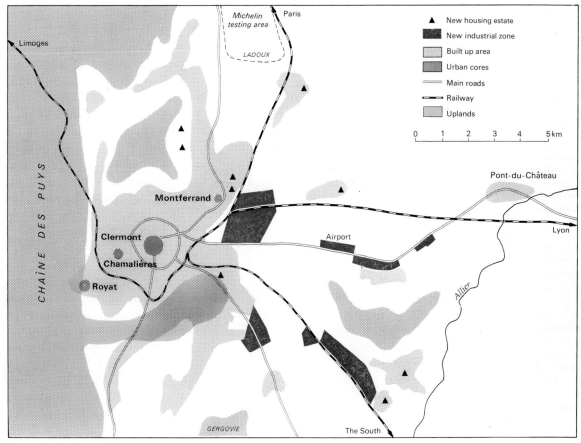

Fig. 16. Clermont-Ferrand

Etienne. Large factories have to be built in the Forez plain north of the city centre. Commuting problems have resulted from this separation of residence and workplace. City planners urge that some redevelopment sites within the built-up area should be used for light industries providing jobs near homes. More housing must be built close to the new industrial estates north of the city. The Berliet vehicle corporation's decision to open a large factory there emphasizes this need. As a result, this northern area has been designated as the major focus for Saint-Etienne's urban expansion programme up to the end of the century.

Clermont-Ferrand

In 1975 the Clermont-Ferrand urban area housed 250 000 inhabitants, 82 per cent more than in 1954 (137 000). Such growth has resulted from the continuing vitality of the rubber industry and the development of a wide range of service facilities for the whole of the Auvergne. To take a single example, the university had only 1000 students on the eve of World War II but more than 15 000 in 1973. Clermont-Ferrand functions as an important reception zone for migrants leaving rural areas of the Massif. Many are young married couples and it is not surprising that birth rates in suburban housing estates and in nearby villages in the Limagnes are the highest in the Massif Central. The demographic dynamism of Clermont-Ferrand and its neighbouring settlements stands in strong contrast with the decline of population elsewhere in the Massif.

Clermont-Ferrand will undoubtedly continue to increase its population in the future and planners are now concerned with managing the whole of the lowland area between Vichy and Issoire to accommodate further expansion. By 1985 the Allier Valley Metropolitan Area will contain between 800 000 and 1 000 000 people. Only 300 000 can be housed in the Clermont-Ferrand conurbation. The remainder will live in expanded towns and new communities elsewhere.

The site conditions of Clermont-Ferrand, with steeply rising ground to the immediate west of the city, will continue to direct new housing and industrial estates eastwards into the Limagnes (Fig. 16). Old suburbs such as Chamalières and Royat are now dependent on the central city for service provision. Land prices are high in these fashionable suburbs which are undergoing important changes as early twentieth century villas are brought up for demolition and high-price apartments constructed in their place. More distant settlements on the edge of the Chaîne des Puys have experienced important growth, but because of steeply rising ground and poor public transport facilities it is unlikely that much more expansion will take place. By contrast, the highest rates of population growth are occurring in an area east of the city centre with vast new housing estates (2000 new dwellings each year during the 1960s), the university's science campus, the new regional hospital, industrial estates, and the regional airport.

In addition to catering for expansion, the city planners of Clermont-Ferrand are tackling urban renovation. In spite of important building programmes since 1955, one-fifth of the conurbation's dwellings date from before 1871. Many need replacement. Living conditions are worst in the medieval city with its tall, tightly-packed houses built of local black lava. Slum areas will be demolished in the near future and replaced by modern housing and commercial premises, as well as badly needed parking facilities. Some areas of old housing are of particular architectural interest and the town centres of Montferrand and Riom are being restored as conservation areas.

Vital road improvements are being undertaken to allow the Allier Valley Metropolitan Area to function successfully in the future. Access between Clermont-Ferrand, its new suburbs, and surrounding settlements is being speeded up as new roads are built. Underpasses will ease traffic flows through the city centre and bypasses allow non-local traffic to skirt round densely built-up areas.

In spite of its size and important recent growth, Clermont-Ferrand was not designated as one of the major regional cities of France (*métropoles d'équilibre*) around which the future planning of the country will be organized. Eight *métropoles* were selected by virtue of their range of service facilities and the size of their hinterland. Clermont-Ferrand came in tenth position. The Massif Central still lacks a focus for administration and planning. It is unlikely that a comprehensive management plan will ever be drawn up for the whole region.

Modern development in Clermont-Ferrand

French Government Tourist Office

5 The Future of the Massif Central

The Massif Central can be divided into three main parts: first, the basins of the Allier and the Loire where important urban growth is taking place and agriculture is being modernized; second, a number of smaller urban foci which act as 'holding points' for economic activities; and third, the vast mountain backbone where population is declining. A comparison of the results of the two most recent censuses supports this generalization. The population of the Massif Central increased by 3 per cent between 1962 and 1975, compared with 13 per cent for the whole of France. Growth was recorded in *départements* which contained large cities (Haute-Vienne, Loire, Puy-de-Dôme) or were located on the eastern margins of the Massif Central (Ardèche) that had benefited from industrial decentralization. Net losses were recorded in southern and central *départements*. A finer degree of analysis shows that villages were rapidly losing their resident population, which was migrating to local market towns and to major employment centres in and beyond the Massif Central.

Forecasting change is always a hazardous business, but by considering recent trends in European society it is possible to suggest that the resources of the Massif Central and other upland areas in Europe will be used differently in the 1980s and beyond. The agricultural population will decrease rapidly as elderly farmers die or retire and are replaced by fewer young men. The settlement network will be thinned out. Some hamlets and isolated farms will become completely deserted. Other settlements will survive only because most of their houses will be bought up by city dwellers for second homes or retirement cottages. Schools, shops, and medical services will be increasingly concentrated in key villages and market towns, which will hold or even increase their population. The age structure of the rural population will probably not change significantly since the tendency is for elderly

Areas in the Puy-de-Dôme are now systematically afforested under the guidance of the SOMIVAL
French Government Tourist Office

people to live longer and more of them will choose to retire to the countryside. By contrast, growth zones in the Allier Valley, around Limoges, and to the north of Saint-Etienne will become more congested with larger concentrations of people, houses, factories, and offices.

Important changes will stem from increased personal mobility. Already one French family in two owns a car. It will not be long before virtually every family will own a car and many will possess more than one. Such a trend will have three important implications. First, most rural residents, whether farmers or retired people, will be able to drive to 'holding points' to obtain services. Second, urbanites will have the opportunity of living at greater distances from their places of work. In any case the length of the average working day and working week will be shortened. The attractions of living in a country house and having a fairly long drive to work on three or four days each week will be even greater. Commuting hinterlands around employment centres will be broadened as the city becomes dispersed into the countryside. This process will intensify as a result of the third trend, which is for city dwellers to spend their weekends and holidays in second homes in the countryside. Many empty farmhouses will be purchased and renovated for this purpose. More estates of second homes will be built.

Extra recreational facilities for city dwellers will be installed. Hydro-electric power reservoirs will be used for sailing and water skiing and will be ringed by chalets. More valleys will be flooded for recreation lakes and the winter snowfields will be exploited even further. As a result of policies for agricultural rationalization wide stretches of country will be set aside as national or regional parks around the Allier Valley, Saint-Etienne, and in the depopulated south of the Massif. Northern areas, such as the Morvan and upland parts of Allier *département*, will become weekend suburbs for Parisians. However, recreation cannot completely replace farming as a use for land. Weekenders and holidaymakers enjoy seeing tidy landscapes rather than ones which have been invaded by rough grass and scrub. In the future some 'farmers' will have to be subsidized as 'park keepers'.

Other rural areas will lose their agricultural activities and some parts of the Massif Central, such as the plateaux of Limousin, that have few landscape attractions for weekenders will be planted up with trees. Smaller zones of woodland in closer proximity to large cities will be used for picnicking and walking as well as for timber production. Agricultural activities will be concentrated in areas with the best physical potential for producing crops or livestock. Arable farming will occupy only a very small proportion of land since it will no longer be able to compete with production from large, mechanized farms in the Paris Basin. Remaining agricultural areas in the mountains will be used for fodder production and fattening beef cattle on large, ranch-like farms.

Links between town and country in the Massif Central will be strengthened and city dwellers will move back to the countryside on a seasonal and weekend basis. The population of some communities will be stabilized as elderly urbanites convert their second homes for permanent occupation in retirement. It is unlikely that the Massif Central and other European uplands that lack Alpine snows will be able to attract large numbers of foreign tourists for their vacations. Sunnier climates in southern Europe, package tours, and the ease of long-distance jet travel to more distant parts of the world will prevent that.

This scenario was devised before the implications of the oil crisis of 1973 fuelled inflation, cooled Western economies and, of particular relevance here, raised doubts about the future of car ownership for the bulk of the population. Now, in the late 1970s, the future seems likely to be rather less dismal than was being predicted a few years ago. Personal mobility will continue to increase but perhaps less dramatically than was believed in the 1960s. As a result, the impact of commuting, recreation, and retirement on the countryside will be rather more muted. The resources of the countryside of central France will be reappraised with every fluctuation in economic health as well as every change in fashion and lifestyle.

As we have seen, a wide range of planning action has been taken in the Massif Central in recent years, but in May 1975 Valery Giscard d'Estaing could report that the region was far from being sufficiently developed to allow the majority of its inhabitants, and especially its young people, to realize their job and lifestyle aspirations within the Massif. Forty proposals for the future were made and these focused on the following objectives: to break down the region's isolation (by financing the construction of new roads and modernizing railway stock, local airports, and the telephone service); to encourage the installation of new manufacturing industries; to modernize farming, forestry, craft activities, and mining; and to enhance the services and facilities available in the region's small and medium-sized towns.

Further Work

The regional geography of the Massif Central is presented in:

MONKHOUSE, F. J. *A Regional Geography of Western Europe*, Longmans, London, 1959 and later editions: chapter 20.

ORMSBY, H. *France: a Regional and Economic Geography*, Methuen, London, 1931 and later editions: chapter 2.

Recent social and economic problems are discussed in:

CLOUT, H. D. *The Geography of Post-War France*, Pergamon Press, Oxford, 1972: chapter 10.

THOMPSON, I. B. *Modern France: a Social and Economic Geography*, Butterworths, London, 1970: chapters 27 and 28.

Work in English includes:

BIRD, J. H. 'Road and rail in the Massif Central in France', *Annals of the Association of American Geographers*, **44**, 1954, pp. 1–14.

CLOUT, H. D. 'Rural improvements in Auvergne', *Geography* **53**, 1968, pp. 79–81.

—'Problems of rural planning in the Auvergne', *Planning Outlook*, **6**, 1969, pp. 29–37.

—'Auvergne—a challenge for country planners', *Geographical Magazine*, **41**, 1969, pp. 918–26.

—'Limousin: regional crisis and change', *Tijdschrift voor Economische en Sociale Geografie*, **61**, 1970, pp. 288–99.

—'Social aspects of second-home occupation in the Auvergne', *Planning Outlook*, **9**, 1970, pp. 33–49.

—'Second homes in the Auvergne', *Geographical Review*, **61**, 1971, pp. 530–53.

—'Part-time Farming in the Puy-de-Dôme département', *Geographical Review*, **62**, 1972, pp. 271–3.

—'Agricultural plot consolidation in the Auvergne region', *Norsk Geografisk Tiddskrift*, **28**, 1974, pp. 181–94.

—'Population changes in the Auvergne region', *Erdkunde*, **28**, 1974, pp. 246–59.

—'Structural reform in French farming: the case of the Puy-de-Dôme', *Tijdschrift voor Economische en Sociale Geografie*, **66**, 1975, pp. 234–45.

HOUSE, J. W. 'A comparative study of landscapes in the Plateau de Millevaches and the western Cevennes', *Transactions, Institute of British Geographers*, **20**, 1954, pp. 154–80.

SCARGILL, D. I. *The Dordogne Region*, David & Charles, Newton Abbot, 1974.

The following articles and books in French are most useful:

BOZON, P. 'Saint-Etienne et son agglomération', *L'Information Géographique*, **37**, 1973, pp. 130–41.

BRUNET, R. 'Organisation de l'espace et cartographie de modèles: les villes du Massif Central', *L'Espace Géographique*, **1**, 1972, pp. 43–8.

ESTIENNE, P. and JOLY, R. *Les Régions du Centre*, Presses Universitaires de France, Paris, 1961.

ESTIENNE, P. 'Clermont-Ferrand en 1973', *L'Information Géographique*, **36**, 1972, pp. 209–20.

DERRUAU-BONNIOL, S. and FEL, A. *Le Massif Central*, Presses Universitaires de France, Paris, 1963.

DERRUAU, S. and ESTIENNE, P. 'Evolution récente du Massif Central français', *L'Information Géographique*, **29**, 1965, pp. 148–57, 185–93.

FEL, A. *L'Auvergne et le Bourbonnais*, Larousse, Paris, 1973.

SCHNETZLER, J. 'Le bassin houiller de la Loire', *L'Information Géographique*, **30**, 1966, pp. 110–18.

—'Saint-Etienne', *Revue de Géographie Alpine*, **57**, 1969, pp. 295–323.

Valuable material is contained in the appropriate French regional geographical journals:

1. Auvergne: *Revue d'Auvergne* (also known as *Travaux de l'Institut de Géographie de Clermont-Ferrand*);
2. Eastern margins: *Revue de Géographie Alpine* and *Revue de Géographie de Lyon*;
3. Limousin: *Norois;*
4. Southern margins: *Bulletin de la Société Languedocienne de Géographie*;
5. South-western areas: *Revue Géographique des Pyrénées et du Sud-Ouest.*

Each article in these journals is abstracted in the appropriate series of *Geographical Abstracts*. Periodicals may be purchased from: Geo Abstracts, University of East Anglia, Norwich, NR4 7TJ.

Index